ENDORSEMENTS

"I like this book. The content is informative and interesting. Father Angus' exploration into the influence of Jesus of Nazareth on Judaism, Christianity, and Islam is both brilliant and compelling reading. Did I say, "Influence on Judaism?" Yes! You must read it! It may be disturbing to some readers, but it is potentially a good ice-breaker for conversation and peace making."

Lloyd L. Hyde, Former publisher of Jamaica-West Indian America Magazine & Consul of Jamaica in Chicago and the Midwest USA

"This book opens a window through which the reader may see and understand the development of religions and cultures. Despite the common interest in business and economic development of Jews, Christians, and Muslims, the expectation of social scientists that religions would unite people has been frustrated. The unanswered question remains – "Why can't we unite?" This book attempts to answer that question.

— Verley Harrison, a former associate at the Bank of Jamaica. Currently an international business consultant in Canada and the Caribbean.

"That Jesus, the man from Nazareth, who I have worshipped as the Son of God, is also the second most important prophet of Islam, is jaw dropping information. Dr. Angus' *God Empties "Self" Into A Man*, is a potential game changer in the relationship of Jews, Christians, and Muslims. My Christianity is much enhanced knowing that "God slid into the womb of a virgin, and that Mary is truly the mother of God." Highly recommended reading.

> Laxley Rodney, PhD; Research Professor, Education Leadership.

GOD EMPTIED "SELF" INTO A MAN

GOD EMPTIED "SELF" INTO A MAN

Jesus of Nazareth in Judaism, Christianity, And Islam

J. Lloyd Angus

"God was in Christ Reconciling the World unto Himself."

II Cor. 5:19

EQUIP PRESS

Colorado Springs

GOD EMPTIED
"SELF"
INTO A MAN

Copyright © 2019, J. Lloyd Angus

All rights reserved. No part of this publication may be reproduced, distributed, or transmitted in any form or by any means, without prior written permission.

Published by Equip Press, Colorado Springs, CO

"Unless otherwise noted, all Bible quotes in this text are attributed to the King James version."

Scripture quotations marked (ESV) are taken from The ESV® Bible (The Holy Bible, English Standard Version®) copyright © 2001 by Crossway, a publishing ministry of Good News Publishers. ESV® Text Edition: 2011. The ESV® text has been reproduced in cooperation with and by permission of Good News Publishers. Unauthorized reproduction of this publication is prohibited. Used by permission. All rights reserved.

Scripture quotations marked (KJV) are taken from the King James Bible. Accessed on Bible Gateway at www.BibleGateway.com.

Scripture quotations marked (NASB) are taken from the New American Standard Bible® (NASB), copyright © 1960, 1962, 1963, 1968, 1971, 1972, 1973, 1975, 1977, 1995 by The Lockman Foundation, www.Lockman.org. Used by permission.

Scripture quotations marked (NIV) are taken from the Holy Bible, New International Version. Copyright © 1973, 1978, 1984, 2011 by Biblica, Inc.® Used by permission. All rights reserved worldwide.

Scripture quotations marked (NKJV) are taken from the New King James Version®. Copyright © 1982 by Thomas Nelson, Inc. Used by permission. All rights reserved.

Scripture quotations marked (NLT) are taken from the Holy Bible, New Living Translation, copyright © 1996, 2004, 2015 by Tyndale House Foundation. Used by permission of Tyndale House Publishers, Inc., Carol Stream, Illinois 60188. All rights reserved.

Scripture quotations marked (NRSV) are taken from the New Revised Standard Version Bible, copyright © 1989 the Division of Christian Education of the National Council of the Churches of Christ in the United States of America. Used by permission. All rights reserved.

First Edition: 2019

God Emptied "Self" into a Man / J. Lloyd Angus

Paperback ISBN: 978-1-946453-67-9

eBook ISBN: 978-1-946453-68-6

EQUIP PRESS

Colorado Springs

Carey & Mary-Ellen

Joslyn/Floyd/Sherwin

Vincent Dia

Theron & Frances

Rita Angus

Valerie Hinckley

IN WHICH OF THE ABOVE IMAGES MAY GOD BECOME HUMAN TODAY?

CONTENTS

	Acknowledgement	11
	Preface	15
1.	Jesus Pre-Existed Judaism, Christianity, And Islam	23
2.	Who Is Jesus of Nazareth?	31
3.	The Meaning of the Word "God"	35
4.	Particularism	41
5.	Religion: What Is It?	49
6.	The Timeline of Abrahamic Religious Emergence	57
7.	Judeo-Christian Scriptures As Salvation History	61
8.	God Is the One Great Mystery	67

JUDAISM — 69

9.	Judaism: Could Jesus of Nazareth Be the Son of God?	79
10.	Is Jesus A Jewish Prophet And/Or A Zealot?	83
11.	Jewish Monotheism And Christian Trinitarianism	89
12.	Perspective of Judaism: Was There A Historical Jesus (Christ) of Nazareth?	93

CHRISTIANITY — 99

13.	Ecumenical Councils	115
14.	Summary of the Seven Ecumenical Councils And Their Mandates	139
15.	The Consistency of Christology	143
16.	Who Killed Jesus? Perspective of Christianity	147

ISLAM	**151**
17. Nativity of Jesus in the Qur'an	161
18. Jesus of Nazareth: The Prophet of Islam	169
19. Jesus of Nazareth in Christianity And Islam: Differences And Similarities	179
20. Islamic Perspective: Who Killed Jesus?	183
21. The Future of Jesus Christ In Islam	187
Postlude	197
Postscript	209
Endnotes	215
Author's Biography	223

ACKNOWLEDGEMENT

I am a gift from God to hardworking yeoman farmers and business people who networked with likeminded self-motivated yeoman farmers and business people, government employed professionals, and seminary-trained Anglican, Baptist, and Presbyterian clergymen. Their examples and nurture enabled me to successfully navigate the complex communities of academia and work, and to chart the trajectory of my personal and professional growth.

I continuously see and feel the hand of God in my interactions with clerical and lay colleagues in my ministry. They guided, nurtured, and scripted me to become the caring Christian pastor and reflective scholar and intellectual that I have become. I credit the direction and reach of my spiritual journey to them.

Many asked about my call to ministry and about my spiritual quest. Some seemed disappointed when I said that it did not come as an altar call or a response to a great sermon. It was a response to the human faces of God in the Church. A front-page story in a newspaper raised my consciousness to the fact that the Church is a mirror to a caring God. The government's well-intentioned bulldozing of a shanty town for urban renewal in the spring of 1962 failed to heed the maxim, "Make haste slowly." Mothers with young children who were victims of the bulldozing made do with tombs as their bed in the sprawling May Pen cemetery of crime ridden western Kingston, Jamaica. The churches loaned invaluable fallowed acreage on the outskirt of the city in response to the groans of terrified mothers and hollering children. The military pitched tents and built the necessary sanitary infrastructure to decently shelter the homeless poor. It was ironic that two institutions which relevance I had hitherto questioned looked heroic. The church and the military felt very welcoming to me thereafter. I was willing to die with them.

I am a cradle Anglican. I was baptized in St. George's Anglican Church and Mt. Nebo Baptist Church. I had some wonderful spiritual experiences with the Boys' Brigade at Mt. Nebo Baptist Church and tagged along with classmates in Kingston to St. George's and St. Matthew's Anglican, Holy Trinity Roman Catholic Cathedral, and some evening worship at churches whose names escape my memory. Differences pulled and pushed and formed my spirituality.

The Reverend A. Oliver Frazer at Mt. Nebo Baptist is special to me. The presence of his wife and himself at the wedding of one of my three sons in Ocho Rios, Jamaica, gave me great pleasure. He was pastor to my maternal grandmother after the death of her diehard Anglican husband. I modeled much of my spiritual development on his demeanor and personality. The Reverend Clement Thomas, the one-time general-secretary of the United Church (Presbyterian) of Jamaica and Grand Cayman counseled me on the virtue of patience, and not to align myself with avant-garde and disgruntled clergy whose fellowship and support I felt were important. He encouraged my intellectual development and gave me a wonderful reference when I migrated to the United States. Last, but not least, the Right Reverend Quinten E. Primo, Jr., Bishop-Suffragan of Chicago (Episcopal) who sponsored me into the USA and the Episcopal Church, USA in 1975. He researched my background surreptitiously after a seminary colleague and a Diocese of Chicago resident cleric with whom I studied Athanasius and Anselm at McCormick Theological Seminary suggested to him that the Diocese of Chicago recruit me for service in the Episcopal Church, USA. The cleric was privy to information that I was in a serious accident on a Jamaica mountain road and may be amenable to relocation to the Prairies of the USA. He probably sensed my paranoia about driving on the precipitous mountainous terrain of that region.

I deeply appreciate the men and women who guided my spiritual development in Jamaica, Grand Cayman, and in the United States of America where I served, and who tolerated my pastoral and pulpit mediocrity. Special thanks to the people who welcomed me to Chicago. They were mindful of my frustration getting acclimated to the big city. They encouraged me and assured me of their prayers.

To the people in Falmouth-Mt. Zion-Barrett Town; Spaulding-Mt. Olivet-Alston, Jamaica; Bodden Town, Northside, East End, and Gun Bay in Grand Cayman; and Chicago, Illinois; Jacksonville, Florida; and Savannah, Georgia, thanks. You have been the hands and eyes of God to me. We were mutually motivated to be co-servants with Jesus of Nazareth.

I began writing this story in coastal South Carolina. There were five pages of end notes when I began editing it. I lost them in the processes of saving my edits. I spent much time recreating the end notes for publication. I apologize should there be any borrowed material that is not acknowledged in the end notes.

Thanks to my wife, Rita Sylvia, for her patience and support throughout this process and for being a sounding board for ideas. She also read sections of the manuscript. Thanks also to my sons Joslyn, Jr., (Josh), Floyd, and Sherwin; Vincent Dia, Mr. & Mrs. Carey Mandeville (Mary Ellen), Mr. & Mrs. Theron Dill (Frances Cho), and Mrs. Valerie Hinkley, saints militant at St. David's Episcopal Church in Columbia, South Carolina, for giving permission to use their photographs as icons of what "God" may be like should "He" become human in this generation.

PREFACE

GOD IS A LIVING MAN: JESUS OF NAZARETH IN JUDAISM, CHRISTIANITY, AND ISLAM

Meeting and knowing people had always been a passion of mine. I believed that the best way to know people is to hear their stories as they tell it. I interacted with the first wave of refugees flowing out from Cuba and filtered through Jamaica where they were screened by the consular staff at the Embassy of the United States of America in Kingston, Jamaica, for entry into the United States of America. They were honored guests at the YMCA residences. They were from Cuba's land and business gentry. I listened to late-night national propaganda broadcasts on BBC, Voice of America, Radio Moscow, Bulgarian National Radio, among others. Traveling abroad, I sought out people who were apparently from third-world countries and alone. I initiated conversations with them. I spent much time listening to whoever seemed highly motivated to tell his or her story.

My initial years as a student of theology were dedicated to the study of biblical languages and the early fathers of the Christian church. I did Biblical Hebrew, koine Greek, Patristic church history, and the Judeo-Christian Testaments in preparation for the preliminary examination which is a prerequisite qualifying test to write the examination for the Bachelor of Divinity degree at the University of London. I did Ecclesiastical Latin later at another academy. Hebrew was the most challenging of the languages I studied. Apart from being read from right to left, Hebrew was without vowels, until vowel pointing was added to the Masoretic text after the sixth century. I learned that the consonants in the names Joshua and Jesus meant liberator or savior. Joshua saved or liberated the Israelites from the ravaging attacks of their neighbors in Palestine.[i] Jesus of Nazareth liberate humans from their sins. In preparation for His incarnation, God sent the angel Gabriel to a young virgin, Mary, with the message:[ii]

"You will conceive and give birth to a son, and you are to call him Jesus."

The Gospel according to Matthew reads, [iii]

"She will give birth to a son, and you are to give him the name Jesus, because
He will save his people from their sins."

This happened in the Roman province of Palestine, when Tiberius (Caesar) was the Emperor, and when

Pontius Pilate was governor or proconsul of Judah, and Herod was tetrarch of Galilee, and Annas and Caiaphas were the high priests. A young woman of impeccable moral character became pregnant while still being a virgin. She delivered a baby boy and named him Jesus. Although Jesus referred to himself as the "Son of Man" 80 times in the four Canonical Gospels of the Christian Church, the Gospel according to John implied that he is God.[iv] The first theologian of Christianity, Paul of Tarsus, referred to him as the "Son of God" in his first sermon in a synagogue in Damascus.[v]

This book is an introduction to the story of Jesus Christ of Nazareth. It casts Him as the centerpiece of Christianity--a person which the prophets of the Jewish Scriptures anticipated and Muslims revered as a prophet who foretold the rising of another prophet, the prophet Mohammad.

Secular society continues to ask, "Who is Jesus of Nazareth?" Was He a historic person or a mere figment of the imagination of a cultic community? Was He God or a messenger from God? What did He believe about God and about Himself? How, why, and for what did He die? Was He the Messiah foretold by the prophets of Israel? Could He be the God-man?

Christians and Muslims believe and teach that Jesus of Nazareth is historical. The two faiths revere Him but in different ways. Both believe that He is the Messiah or Christ. Christianity teaches that Jesus is more than a man who God anointed. Christians believe that Jesus of Nazareth is God and the Son of God. He is God with us, the "Emanuel. He rose to life again after they crucified Him, and He is the model for the familiar pictures and statues of Him that adorn churches, monasteries, and museums. He fulfills the messianic prophesies of the Jewish prophets.[vi]

This book is written from the perspective of a Christian who has explored Christianity as an Anglican, a Roman Catholic, a Baptist, a Presbyterian, and is a practicing Anglican (Episcopal Church, USA). I believe that God became the living, historical man called Jesus of Nazareth.

I have been exposed to Judaism and Islam. I had been a guest at Jewish cult rituals including a Bar Mitzvah and a Holy Day observance at a synagogue in Jacksonville, Florida, and I co-presided with a gracious rabbi at a Christian-Jewish wedding at a synagogue in Roswell, Georgia. My experience of Islam is limited to visits to the Nation of Islam's Mosque in Chicago and to a mosque in Uganda, East Africa, in the company of two Church of Uganda clergymen. I also observed Muslims praying at airports in East Africa and Eastern Europe and infiltrated a Muslim Festival on the bank of the Danube in Belgrade, Serbia. Serbian Orthodox Christians are seemingly still traumatized or want to perpetuate their historic anxiety of Turkish Muslim raiders. They post manikins of Serbian soldiers at entrances of some ancient church buildings as a reminder.

Jews believe that Jesus of Nazareth, the Son of Mary, was a non-descript zealot and messianic pretender. He is

Lord and God to Christians. He is the revered prophet of Islam and the center of interest of this reflection. Despite the disagreement of the three Abrahamic faiths: Judaism, Christianity, and Islam, they may be unwittingly worshipping the same God (YHWH-Elohim-Allah. Social theorist and economist Stuart Chase aptly sums up the situation with the maxim:

*"For those who believe, no proof is necessary,
for those who don't believe, no proof is possible."*[vii]

I hope that this introductory monogram will facilitate meaningful conversations about Jesus of Nazareth wherever people gather. A three-fold strategy is suggested.

i. An examination of the core beliefs of Judaism, Christianity, and Islam.
ii. Exploration to determine the history of their cultural and theological divergence.
iii. Determine the peace-making benefits of the dialogue.

The Abrahamic religions account for over 3.8 billion of the 7.5 billion inhabitants of the earth. This study refers to them as the Abrahamic people because their history as religious communities has a common trajectory. The numerical estimates of the three principal Abrahamic cults are: [viii]

Christianity	*Approximately two billion, two hundred and forty million.*
Islam	*Approximately one billion, six hundred and ten million.*
Judaism	*Approximately fourteen million*

Unfortunately, they have coexisted as combatants for almost 1,400 years. Their combativeness has done much collateral damage to non-combatants along the way.

Constantinople, the capital of the Byzantine (Orthodox) Christian Empire, fell to the Muslim Turks in the Spring of 1453. Christianity apparently has military and economic hegemony over Islam in the 20th and 21st centuries. Large Muslim populations were under mandated colonial rule of countries which were allied members of the United Nations at the end of the Second World War. Given the economic and military hegemony of the Christian countries with mandated powers, Islam incubated as a repressed faith of colonial subjects for many years. Christians were therefore perceived as oppressors, and the Muslim populations retreated to their mosques in righteous indignation, where a socio-political Islamic Fundamentalism developed. The Jewish Diaspora also generate anger. Many ask whether there would have been a Jewish Holocaust by the Nazi Germany without the complicity of Christian ecclesiastical institutions. Their apparent complicity harrowed the conscience of Christian Europe. They have since been perpetually apologizing and large numbers have abandoned religious faith. Some former colonial people, notably the political leaders of

Guyana, which is on the northeast coast of South America, elevated indigenous and ethnic religions to parity and legal status with Christianity.

Despite Jesus' place of honor in the Qur'an, Muslims who were subjects of European Christian suzerains are less inclined to refer to Jesus in their discourse. That may be an emotional reaction to the denigration of the prophet Mohammad and Islam by Christian colonists.

The Jewish philosopher and theologian Martin Buber reflected on the myopia of the human being wrote:[ix]

> *"When we walk our way and encounter a man who comes towards us, walking his way, we know our way only and not his; for he comes to life for us only in the encounter"*

The encounter, unfortunately, oftentimes happen with the intensity and savagery of wild male beasts in the mating season.

This book is non-sectarian. Instead of the timeline of Christendom, B.C. and A.D., I chose the format adopted by academia and global commerce. That timeline uses the format: Before the Common Era (B. C. E.) and the Common Era (C. E.).

GOD EMPTIED "SELF" INTO A MAN

1

JESUS PRE-EXISTED JUDAISM, CHRISTIANITY, AND ISLAM

"By faith Abraham, when he was called, obeyed by going out to a place which he was to receive for an inheritance and went out not knowing where he was going."
[Heb. 11:8 AV]

Jews, Christians, and Muslims have this common testimony of their faith. They believe that God called Abraham (Abram) when he was already 75 years old and still living in Mesopotamia, and commanded him to take his wife, his servants, and his herds and embark on an uncharted mission.[x] They believe that Abram trusted God and obeyed the divine command unconditionally. With his extended family in tow, he traveled to wherever God directed him. He went through Palestine into Egypt and back to Palestine.

Abraham bought Hagar, a female slave, while in Egypt and gave her to his wife, Sarai (Sarah), to be her maidservant. Sarai, who had difficulty conceiving, followed a traditional practice, gave Hagar to Abram as a surrogate to conceive a child to be their heir. Hagar conceived and gave birth to Ishmael. Sarai conceived later and gave birth to Isaac. Isaac had one son, Jacob. Jacob had twelve sons. One of Jacob's sons, Joseph, became the grand vizier of the Pharaoh in Egypt. He managed the granaries of Egypt, and thereby got the pharaoh to settle his father Jacob and his 11 brothers on prime grazing land in Goshen, Egypt. After much trials and tribulations, the descendants of Abraham were enslaved along with other foreign ethnics then living in Egypt. According to Old Testament scholar John Bright, the foreign ethnics were known as "Abiru or Apiru,"[xi] which apparently became known as Hebrews.

The Judeo-Christian Scriptures are stories of liberation. God called and sent Moses to liberate the Hebrews after about four hundred years as slaves in Egypt. God revealed the Divine Name to Moses as, "I am who I am." The Hebrew word for "I am who I am" is YHWH. YHWH can also be translated as: "*I am what I am,*" "*I will be what I will be.*" John Topel of Seattle University in a bi-centennial lecture added "*I create what I create,*" and "*Mystery! I will not tell you my name keep following me and find out.*"[xii] Judaism, Christianity, and Islam believe that God, YHWH, is perpetually and continuously active with human beings in history.

YHWH is the God of Israel and El was the name of the senior God in Mesopotamia and Palestine. Elohim, El Shaddai, and El Roi were also names of God in Israel. They were apparently used interchangeably with YHWH.

The names "Shaddai, and Roi" modify the name "El." El Shaddai was therefore "God almighty or god of the mountain. "Allah," on the other hand, is an Arabic word for God. The name "Allah" predates Islam and is the Arabic word used also by Arabic speaking Christians and other religious sects as the name of God. An alternate name of God in Arabic is the variant of Allah, namely "Elaha or Alaha."

Christians believe that God became a human being — the man Jesus of Nazareth. That is referred to as the divine incarnation of God becoming flesh. Jesus is the incarnation (in-flesh form) of YHWH. The Incarnation of God as man is a mystery. The annunciation of the angel Gabriel to Mary suggests that it was non-sexual process, [xiii]

> *"The Holy Spirit will come on you, and God's power will rest upon you. For this reason the Holy Child will be called the Son of God."*
> **(Luke 1:35 Good News Version)**

The annunciation to Joseph reflects a similar non-sexual conception,

> *"Joseph, descendant of David, do not be afraid to take Mary to be your wife. For it is by the Holy Spirit that she has conceived. She will have a son, and you will name him Jesus — because he will save his people from their sins.*
> **(Matthew 1:20 – 21, Todays English Version)**

The story of the incarnation in the Gospel according to John (John 1:1 & 14) is modest and appropriate for faith formation of adults and minors alike. The phrasing of the Johannine incarnation, *"The Word was God"* and *"The Word became a human being and . . . lived among us,"* succinctly expresses the mystery that God becomes a living human being. The word "Word" in that text (John 1:1) is the English translation of the Greek, "(Logos) Logos" and refers to the Essence of Divinity; the essence of being God.

The nativity or birth stories in the Gospels according to Matthew and Luke suggests that YHWH's humbled state became a zygote after it took up residence in the womb of Mary and gestated there with a human body from Mary. Because whatever God touches becomes holy, the incarnation could happen in any womb, but Christianity and Islam believe that God prepared Mary to be the mother of Jesus. The Islamic Tradition is that God gave Mary as a special child to her parents Joachim and Anne.

Most Christians believe that although Mary gave birth vaginally to the God-Man Jesus of Nazareth, she was perpetually a virgin. The Church struggled to develop a statement that fully expressed its faith that Jesus of Nazareth was a perfect union of human and divine without confusion of natures at seven Ecumenical Councils. The seven Ecumenical Councils were: The First Council of Nicaea (325 C.E); the First Council of Constantinople (381 C E.); the Council of Ephesus (431 C.E.), the Council of Chalcedon (451 C.E.); the Second Council of Constantinople in 553 C.E.; the Third Council of Constantinople in 680 – 681 C.E.; and the Second Council of Nicaea in 787 C.E.[xiv] The mandates of the Councils were announced as decisions, but were oftentimes enforced by imperial fiat.

God (YHWH) is manifested in the Scriptures of Judaism as cloud and smoke or fire and light. The Hebrews going through the Sinai Desert followed the cloud by day and the light by night. The smoke that filled the cavernous Temple, which Solomon built, was believed to be a manifestation of YHWH's presence and pleasure at the dedication of the Temple (2 Chron. 7:1). John the Divine also had a vision of a temple in heaven filled with smoke (Rev. 15:8). The manifestations of YHWH in the Sinai and in the Temple is probably the same God that was revealed in the Book (Kitab) to Mohammad.

The seeming plurality of the names of God in Judaism and Islam do not suggest a college or pantheon of gods but a plurality of manifestations of the One God. There are, however, textual ambiguities that suggest an acknowledgement by Judaism that YHWH is One among other gods, and that YHWH may be head of a pantheon (Psalm 86:8, 96:4, 97:7, 135:5).

Initially, Christianity had difficulty defining the person and nature of God. It was plagued by what is referred to as the Antiochene heresy. That heresy emphasized the distinction of the human and the divine in the person of Jesus of Nazareth. It suggests that Jesus was adopted by God. The Alexandrians, on the other hand, emphasized the perfect union between the human and the divine natures. The Alexandrians explained the union of the humanity and the divinity of Jesus Christ allegorically. Nestorius was a monk in Antioch before he was made the bishop of Constantinople. That explains his stubborn rejection of the mandate of the Council of Ephesus that Mary was the mother of God or (Θεοτοκοσ/Theotokos). He refused to accept the Council's mandate and was exile to a region outside of the Roman Empire, probably in the Sahara or Arabia. It may have laid the theological groundwork for Islam.

In the year 610 C. E., 178 years after Nestorius was exiled from Constantinople, the archangel Gabriel appeared to Mohammad while he was at a mountain retreat near Mecca. Mohammad reported that he was taken to heaven, where the archangel recited the Kitab (Book in heaven) to him. He, in turn, recited it verbatim to his scribes who copied it. That book became the Qur'an, which is the Scriptures of Islam.

Islam teaches that Mary or Maryam is the "Christotokos" or mother of the Messiah (Christ), and that Jesus is the penultimate prophet. It also teaches that Islam was the religion of the Patriarchs. Its primary dogma or "Tawhid" is that "God is One" and that Mohammad is the prophet that God sent to restore it.

For this reflection, the word God, written with an upper-case "G" refers to the God of Judaism, Christianity, and Islam and may be the cognate of Anselm of Canterbury's "That *than which nothing greater can be conceived.*" God cannot be improved because God is a priori perfect. God is infinite, not created nor limited by time and space, and is different from persons and things. This is supported by systematic theologian Paul Tillich, who taught that God is the ground of all beings but chose to become a human being to bridge the chasm between divinity and humanity. Taught also by Oxon's John MacQuarrie, who defines **Being** as a verbal-noun and that all beings, including a supreme-being, are passible or changeable. Jesus himself said, "*He who comes from the earth belongs to the earth and speaks about earthly matters, but he who comes from heaven is above all.*" (John 3:31) Scriptures affirms the infinity of God (Job 38:1 ff, TEV).

The Prophets of Judaism told Israel and Judah that God demanded faithfulness to Torah and encouraged faithfulness to the Torah. The prophet Jeremiah reinforced hope when he said:

> *"Behold the days are coming, declares the Lord, when I will fulfill the good word which I have spoken concerning the house of Israel and the house of Judah . . . I cause a righteous Branch of David to spring forth; and he shall execute justice and righteousness upon the earth."*
> **Jeremiah 33:14-16 (KJAV)**

Isaiah saw hope and said:

> *"The people who walk in darkness will see a great light; those who live in a dark land, the light will shine on them. . . For a child will be born to us, a son will be given to us; . . . and his name will be called Wonderful Counselor, Mighty God, Eternal Father, and Prince of Peace."*
> **Isaiah 9:2, 6 (KJAV)**

The prophet Malachi saw the apostasy and moral failure of the priests and looked beyond them to a divine messenger who would purify Judaism (Malachi 3:1-4),

> *"But who will be able to endure the day when he comes?*
> *. . . He will be like a strong soap, like a fire that refines metal.*
> *. . . so the Lord's messenger will purify the priests, so that they will bring to the Lord the right kind of offerings".* **Malachi 3:2-3 (TEV)**

Jesus also lambasted the scribes and Pharisees for their hypocrisy, saying:

> *"How terrible for you, teachers of the Law*
> *and Pharisees! You hypocrites! You are like*
> *whitewashed tombs which look fine on the outside*
> *but are full of bones and decaying corpses on the*
> *inside."* **Matthew 23:27 (TEV)**

Because the Scriptures of Judaism were not canonized until 90 C.E., the Scriptures from which Jesus of Nazareth quoted were inclusive of a much wider corpus of contemporary Jewish writings. Given that situation, some of His quotations are outside of the Jewish Canon. The Canon of Christianity was not mandated by a synod or an Ecumenical Council of Christianity. The church adopted the canon with the 27 books that Athanasius of Alexandria authorized for the clergy of the Alexandrian region in his Easter pastoral letter in 367 C.E.

2

WHO IS JESUS OF NAZARETH?

The former archbishop of Canterbury, Rowan Williams, asked what the Church of England may contribute to the Spectrum of the Christian Churches. He answered:

> *"It lays in the dual theological principle . . . incarnational and sacramentalist. God had become human and thereby shown that human nature could carry the divine glory; God had raised the whole of human nature and therefore every man and woman to new dignity, . . . fellowship of Christ's body. . . and so declared all material existence to be potentially charged with the life of God."*[xv]

Christians believe that Jesus of Nazareth, the son of the Virgin Mary is historical. They believe that He preexisted the incarnation and remained fully human and divine thereafter. The Gospel according to John (Christian Canon) expresses the incarnation of God in human flesh perfectly. It reads:

"In the beginning was the Word, and the Word was with God, and the Word was God. . ... And the Word became flesh and dwelt among us, and we beheld his glory, glory as of the only begotten from the Father, full of grace and truth."
John 1:1, 14 (KJAV)

"Word" is a translation of (Greek: Logos) and is the divine intelligence and mind and the controlling principle of the universe. The Logos (Word) became a real human being. Christians believe that God became Jesus of Nazareth, the Alpha and the Omega, or the beginning and the end (Rev. 1:8). Christians also believe that Jesus was crucified, died, buried, and rose from the dead. The incarnation or Christmas mystery, and the crucifixion and resurrection (triduum) are the two most important scenes of the Jesus mystery. He is reported to have ascended to the Father (YHWH) and returned to earth as the Holy Spirit to fill the whole earth with His glory (Pentecost).

The four canonical gospels of Christianity are the primary source of information about Jesus Christ or Jesus of Nazareth. The *Acts of the Apostles* is the history of Christianity in its formative stage. Seminal Christianity was Jesus and his trained cadre of twelve men. One committed suicide out of guilt for betraying Jesus to the Romano-Jewish authorities. Mathias was elected to replace Judas. The disciples (apostles) that Jesus left behind told the good news of Jesus' resurrection to Jews and gentiles alike and kept in touch with letter writing. The letters were later collected and known as epistles. What the apostles taught became the tradition of the Christian Church. That tradition is also referred to as the Apostolic Tradition.[xvi]

Muslims believe and teach that Jesus of Nazareth is the Messiah or Christ and second in importance as a prophet of YHWH-Elohim-Allah only to Mohammad. Christians and Muslims teach that the Christ of faith is also the Jesus of history.

Whereas Jews relegate Jesus of Nazareth to the rank of a dangerous pretender, and Muslims teach that He is only an important prophet and Messiah, Christians believe and teach that He is the Messiah, the Son of God, and God, and that His mother is truly the Mother of God.

A recent convert from Christianity to Judaism, who has a hazy understanding of the history and the theological significance of the letters of Paul, displayed extreme emotions akin to epileptic convulsion when I engaged her in dialogue. She referred to Paul as a "wannabe."

Her enthusiasm is not an unusual behavior of converts. Converts are invariably highly motivated and oftentimes irrational apologists for their new faith. Becoming a new member of a cult is both exciting and intimidating.[xvii]

Jews deny that Jesus is or could be a prophet of Judaism because he did not live within the years specified by Judaism as the age of prophecy. Understandably, the passion of Jesus of Nazareth (John 18 & 19) is, without a doubt, the single most important cause of anti-Semitism. Jews have reasons to downplay the prophetic role of Jesus and more reason to deny His divinity. They have been accused and sometimes seem to accept responsibility for crucifying Jesus of Nazareth. Because the Third Reich in

Germany made them the scapegoat for Germany's post World War I social and economic problems, many of them have been skeptical of the rapprochement of Christians thereafter. Jews that were subject to persecution under Christian despots are more prone to create derogatory legends about Jesus of Nazareth. Many of them refer to him as the "false messiah." Others, who were nurtured in a socio-political climate in which Christians and/or Muslims were cordial to them, refer to Jesus of Nazareth as "the failed messiah." Dr. Amy-Jill Levine, a professor of New Testament at Vanderbilt University, in an online post said:

> *"Just as there is no single Jewish view on most matters, there is no single Jewish view about Jesus of Nazareth: some Jews regard him as a wise rabbi, others view him as a heretic, some find inspiration in his teachings, others take offense at his claims."*[xxviii]

3

THE MEANING OF THE WORD "GOD"

In my interactions with peoples of many cultures, it is apparent to me that people in more primitive and underdeveloped societies are more prone to be religious. The belief in extrasensory perception seems to decrease as people's material and emotional needs are satisfied. It is also true that as a population becomes more educated, especially in the social sciences, they tend to be less interested in mystery and religion. My personal reflection mirrors to me that everybody is simultaneously religious and agnostic. Alfred Edward Taylor said that the Christian's belief in God is a fusion of Greek philosophy and the Hebrew Scriptures. I tested that theory listening to funeral sermons at churches with highly-educated as well as with barely-literate clergy. I have heard much that suggests the human being is a soul and a body, and that the soul leaves the body at death to be with the Lord. I have dialogues with pastors who earnestly want to know whether the "soul" of the decease enters the judgment chamber of God immediately after death or on the "Last Day" according to the Apocalypse of John. Taylor suggests that God, in Greek philosophy, is the supreme and perfect intelligence, and that the Hebrew Scriptures propose that God is the supreme and wholly righteous will.[xix] The rational religious person believes that the creator of nature has prefect intelligence and is worthy of adoration and worship.

The relationship between God and mankind is the relationship of the creator to the creature. God gives order to everything. The human mind reflects the creative power of God and becomes co-creators with God. Egyptian, Jewish, and Greek mythologies imply and suggest that God gives order to human life and society. Thomas Aquinas adds to that his understanding that God is the "First Cause," or that which creates, guides, and changes all things without itself being changed. Anselm, a onetime archbishop of Canterbury, in what is known as the Ontological Argument, said that God is absolute and is "*that than which nothing can be greater.*"

God is beyond human comprehension. Interesting! God is infinite and impassible. Although God cannot be proved by scientific observations in a laboratory, neither can the existence and reality of God be thus disproved. Those who believe in the incarnation of God cite faith-knowledge.

The Judeo-Christian Bible gives a timeline for the creation. It tells us that God created everything in six days and then rested on the seventh day. The creative process is announced,

> *"Then God said, 'And now we will make human beings; they will be like us and resemble us. . . . So God created human being, making them to be like himself."* **Genesis 1:26-27 (GNB-TEV)**

God is referred to as plural. That human beings are created in the image of God is an interesting idea. Was that image physical or spiritual? The creation story (Gen. 2:5-7) and the recreation of Israel from the dry bones that God showed to Ezekiel in the valley had much in common (Ezek. 37:1-8). The clay sculpture became a human being when God transferred life (breath) into it (Gen. 2:7) and the dry bones of Ezekiel (Ezek. 37) were alive only when the wind entered them. Human beings become what they are when they receive the divine spirit. God, therefore, is the source of all life.

The creation stories in the first and second chapters of Genesis reads like the first chapter in a book on evolution. It is referred to as primeval myth and the response is faith knowledge. It explains the process of the evolution of the species. It may read like science fiction, but what is science fiction in one age often becomes non-fiction at another time. Man or human beings are created in the image of God. An image is a likeness. Christianity teaches that Jesus was not created and is not an image of God. He was not similar to god as the Arians taught. He was and is God-- the God-man.

Athanasius of Alexandria, a student of Pauline theology (Romans 5:14-19), tells us that God became man (human) to make the human being divine or god-like.

"For he (Jesus) was made man that we might be made God . . . and he endured the insolence of men that we might inherit immortality."[xx]

Judaism acknowledges that God cannot be known. God told Moses that the divine name is, "I am who I am" or "I shall be who I shall be" or "YHWH". Human beings cannot know God fully. That is the message God sent to Job and his friends (Job 38: 1ff). The name YHWH, refer to as the ***tetragammaton***, was displaced by the more universal name "Elohim" as the name of God in Palestine. The religious Judeans stopped vocalizing the name YHWH in the sixth century B.C.E., citing respect for the name. Adonai, which means "All mighty God or Lord" was read wherever YHWH appears in a text. Vowel points were added to the Masoretic text in the 7th century based on the traditional sounds of the Hebrew words. It was pronounced "Yahweh".

The King James Authorized English Version of the Bible was translated from German and Latin translations of the Hebrew "Old Testament." The German translators substituted "J" for the Hebrew "Yodh" because the German alphabet does not have a "Yodh" sounding letter. The English translators followed the lead of the German and Latin translations. YHWH in Latin became "IHWH". The German became "JHWH". JHWH became "Jehovah" in the King James English version. Roman pontiff Benedict XVI directed Roman Catholics not to read aloud the name YHWH in Hebrew or the vernacular to show solidarity with Jews.

That "God is One" is a dogma of Judaism, Christianity, and Islam. The first and second commandments of the Decalogue (Exodus 20:3-5, KJAV) reads:

> *"You shall have no other gods before Me. You shall not make for yourself an idol, or any likeness of what is in heaven above or on the earth beneath or in the water under the earth. You shall not worship them or serve them; for I, the Lord your God am a jealous God."*

The Canaanites who lived in Palestine when the Hebrews (Israelites) got there were an agrarian people and worshipped a God of agriculture. The name of the god was Baal. Baal means "owner" and husband." It is an interesting name for a god, especially given the Canaanite people's understanding of their relationship to Baal. The people and the land were wives and slaves[xxi] of Baal. They also had multiple images of the Ugaritic fertility mother-goddess Asherah.

The confession of Christians that Jesus of Nazareth pre-existed Abraham, and Isaac, and Moses obviously overwhelms religious Judeans. Moses had an epiphany in the Sinai and he and the Hebrews believed God's name was revealed as YHWH. I am inclined to agree with Leslie Dewart that it does not matter what name we give to God--names are human invention and what humans invent; humans can change. St. Thomas' (Aquinas) wisely advice, "Wise people do not worry about names."[xxii] Wise people, however, know that God is infinite, and that what is impossible for man is possible with God. That YHWH became Jesus of Nazareth is probable.

Judaism and Islam feel that statues of national heroes in public places elicit devotional or cultic responses. Christians understand the anxiety of Jews and Muslims but confess their propensity to trust God to reveal all mysteries. An anonymous 12th century Christian defined God as mystery saying, "A circle whose center is everywhere and whose circumference is nowhere." Jesus of Nazareth was always that center. Ayn Rand may be somewhat pedestrian to refer to God as a being, but his incite that God "is a being beyond man's power to conceive" is on target. Also relevant to the conversation on "From whence comes, and who is Jesus of Nazareth" is a comment of Jewish psychotherapist Victor Frankl, "God is the partner of your most intimate soliloquies".

Some post-modern Roman Catholic and Anglican (Episcopal) churches have simple crosses hanging in their sanctuaries instead of ornate crucifix and Christus rex. The architects and the liturgists are inviting worshippers to be more subjective and imagine themselves being crucified and reigning with the timeless Jesus Christ. The subjectivism symbolizes one of two developments.

i. That the Christian subjects him or herself to bearing the cross with Jesus.

ii. The development of the cult of "Self." This may be stretching the analogy, but it does appear to be a symbol of self-adoration.

4

PARTICULARISM

People and groups are always very concerned with identity. Nationalism grew out of the desire of people to identify with a land and a flag. Kinship is identity with genetic or bloodline. Some people identify with others who look or think like them. People with similar skills or interests group together in guilds, and people join churches and clubs that satisfy their needs. Birds flock with those looking like them. Everyone wants to belong. It makes one feel distinctive and secure.

One's nationality and religion are symbols of identity. Western Europeans and North Americans have traditionally been identified as Christians and Jews. Christians are Baptists, Episcopalians, Lutherans, Reformed, Evangelical Pentecostal, and Roman Catholics, among others. That characterization has not always been true and is demonstrably proven false, given the global migration which accelerated in the 16th century. Islam has had a historic presence in Europe and is global.

The Christian Church credits itself as the great unifier of humanity. The colonization of the Americas,

Asia, and Africa unified peoples of diverse ethnicity, races, and religion, while simultaneously setting the stage for the fragmentation of peoples and cultures. A mixed-race couple sought me out after the pastor of a church they had been attending disinvited them. The pastor told them that the Bible forbade the mixing of the races. The couple was too shocked to ask for the Scripture that forbade miscegenation.

I tried to see what Scriptures he had been reading. He probably had been reading the book of Ezra, and particularly Ezra 10:1-10:

> *"Ezra the priest stood up and spoke to them. He said, 'You have been faithless and have brought guilt on Israel by marrying foreign women. ... Separate yourselves from the foreigners living in our land and get rid of your foreign wives."*
> **Ezra 10:1-10 (TEV)**

When the Assyrian and Babylonians carried the most productive Israelites and Judaeans to Mesopotamia in 722 through 686 B.C.E., they integrated those left behind in Palestine with settlers from the Imperial countries. Many of the Judean exiles to Babylon in 689 and 686 apparently settled in segregated Judean communities, where they studied the Torah and maintained cultural and religious purity. That explains the mandate of Ezra that the returnees from exile separate themselves from the social and religious corrupt Palestinians, lest their religion and morality be contaminated. The separation was to prevent cultural and religious contamination. In a similar vein, the apostle Paul was concerned about Christians marrying non-Christians. He did not encourage the breakup of families even when one spouse is not a believer (I Cor. 15 & 16). He apparently believed that a believing spouse could convert the non-Christian. He was not a xenophobe. He wrote to the Galatians:

> *"So there is no difference between Jews and Gentiles, between slaves and free people, between men and women; you are all one in union with Christ Jesus."*
> **Galatians 3:28 (TEV)**

The Acts of the Apostles addressed the issue of an integrated church. The pastor probably read that Scripture. His concern was probably less about integrated congregations and more about mixed race marriage. He was probably pressured by some members of the congregation to dispatch that couple, lest their presence corrupt the minds of the young people in the congregation. The issue of an integrated kingdom of God was also addressed by Simon Peter in the first discourse in the Acts of the Apostles.

> *"Peter began to speak: 'I now realize that it is true that God treats everyone on the same basis. Those who fear him and do what is right are acceptable to him no matter what race they belong to."*
> **Acts of the Apostles 10:34 & 35 (TEV)**

Christianity forbade religious exclusiveness as socially obnoxious and troubling. That obnoxious behavior may include the inhospitable practice of closed communion, which excludes those who are not specifically confirmed in that denomination from sharing at the Lord's Table.

If God is One, and God is the sole creator, all human beings constitute the one family of God. The Gospel according to John (3:16) tells us that God loves the world, not the church exclusively, and gave His only begotten Son to save those who wants to be saved.

Jews, Christians, and Muslims, individually and collectively, believe that there is one God and that God created everything and all people. It is therefore an obvious scandal that Jews, Christians, and Muslims jostle to posture as the favorite of that one God. The three religious faith groups claim primacy as the people that God called out (ecclesia) and denounce the others as infidels (people without faith).

The following hymn of the Christian Church contradicts exclusivism:

> *"All people that on earth do dwell*
> *Sing to the Lord with cheerful full voice."*[xxiii]

Jesuit Teilhard de Chardin in a written response to his religious superior about his faith, said that he had a vision of a universal faith into which all sectarian religions flow, as do rivulets flowing into the ocean.[xxiv] I am disturbed, however, by his seeming pantheism but understand his angst at the inflated human pride of religious sectarians.

He may be on to something meaningful with his desire to see all religions plunging into the totality of one human belief. Maybe his background as a geologist and paleontologist analyst made him less inclined to the democratic principle of freedom to choose. He finally opted to endorse Christianity.

De Chardin is not alone in his search for a universal Sovereign Lord. Neil Postman who found satisfaction in diversity made a similar choice at the end of his own adventure. He opted to validate science and religion, seeming opposites, after an evaluation of the Church's understanding of cult and culture in the West:

> *"The West has inherited two great and different tales – one biblical and one scientific.... both speak of human frailty and error... Our task, perhaps, is to keep both of these stories alive."*[xxv]

Jews, Christians, and Muslims believe that faith is knowledge. Faith knowledge is expressed as, "I know because I believe." What one believes becomes real knowledge to the believer. It has the aura of reality as does empirical knowledge to the believer. Because Jews, Christians, and Muslims believe intensely that God is One, and that they worship the God that sent Abram (Abraham) from Ur in Mesopotamia, it is apparent that they worship the same God. Moses may have seen an optical illusion in the Sinai when he saw the burning bush and heard a voice from the burning bush. He may even have misinterpreted what the voice said to him. He believed that the voice commissioned him to lead the Hebrews from Egypt and build a nation around the Laws of YHWH. If the God that spoke to Moses is the same God that Christians believe became Jesus of Nazareth, and Muslims believe revealed the Qur'an to Mohammad, the name of God is YHWH/Elohim/Allah. Anselm of Canterbury defined the one God as, "*That than which nothing can be greater*". Jesus Christ, the Son of Mary and Son of God, was obviously thinking of that one God when he said, "*I know him (God) for I come from him, and he sent me*"? *(John 7:29B TEV)*

Thomas Aquinas was probably right when he suggested that the women cleaning the offices of professors at the University of Paris knew God better than did the professors, and William Cowper's troubled mind probably experienced flashes of light from God that were denied to more stable souls. He saw:

> *"God moves in a mysterious way His wonders to perform; He plants His footsteps in the seas and rides upon the storms."*

And had an apocalyptic vision which is common to soldiers in fox holes on battle fields:

> *"Far from the world, O Lord, I flee from strife and tumult far from scenes where Satan wages still his most successful war."*

Simone Weil was probably right when she told John Oesterreicher, a parish priest with whom she consulted on the principles of Christianity, that the central tenets of the Christian mysteries were better expressed by the Greek philosophers than by the New Testament.[xxvi] It is interesting how people across racial, national, geographic, and ethnic divides have similar thoughts and beliefs. YHWH/Elohim/Allah is revealed as God to everyone, God does not have favorites.

5

RELIGION: WHAT IS IT?

Religion has been defined as the belief in, and worship or adoration of, a divinity. According to Clarence R. J. Rivers, effective worship is:

> *"Ultimately dependent on the Spirit of God . . . it is facilitated by two dynamics: dramatic structure and artistic performance. . . To participate soulfully is to give witness to one's faith – not in precepts or concepts, but by revealing the embodied action of God within oneself."*[xxvii]

To worship God or gods is to be religious. Judaism, Christianity, and Islam are Abrahamic religions. Their adherents, Jews, Christians, and Muslims, date their religions to when God called Abram and his wife Sarai from Ur in Chaldea (Mesopotamia) and sent him away to initiate a new community of God's people. Septuagenarians and without children when called them, they thanked God for giving them children to continue their bloodline. They and their children set up altars wherever they traveled to worship God.

Judaism, Christianity, and Islam are religions because they are worshiping communities. Worship may be a natural extension of a child's dependence on parents. It is a gift of God that maintains the sanity of the human being. Psychoanalyst Heinz Kohut observed that his clients had a need to mirror themselves in another person and to idolize someone outside of themselves. He suggested that that need may have begun when, as children, they wanted their parents to mirror to them their self-worth.[xxviii] In adulthood, that need for mirroring develops into a need for merger with the idealized other. That merger brings calmness, cohesion, harmony, and gives strength. Religious cults provide the medium for people in the worshipping communities to mirror their goodness. The mirroring gives them positive feedback as they worship. Rabbis, bishops, priests, ministers, pastors, and imams are the physical media through which worshippers experience the mirroring from God. That feeling of interfacing and merging with another is important in psychology. It is that which makes worship possible. It strengthens those who worship.

The words "cult" and "worship" are used interchangeably. Religious cult liturgies form and shape the aspirations of people. The secret of a culture is indeed the cult of the people. Tony Robbins rightly said that we become what we think about all day long.[xxix] The fact is that we become what we think and practice regularly. was not lost on Queen Elizabeth I of England and her Privy

Council and Parliament. Anglicanism fostered a cult that was unique and necessary to preserve the independence of the Church in England, as well as the British Monarchy.

The Jews believe that YHWH directed Moses from the burning bush at Sinai to,

> *'Go in and possess the land which the Lord swore to give to your fathers.'*[xxx]

The Israelites believed that God commissioned them to be the priest nation to the world. They have acted out that role and have successfully convinced many non-Jews that they are God's via media to all worshipping communities. Evangelical Christians, including African-American evangelicals, celebrate their deliverance from Egypt and hate whoever they perceive to be enemies of the Jewish people. Jews faithfully celebrate sabbath, a word which means "cease". They cease working and rest on the seventh day every week to honor their faith-knowledge that God (Gen. 2:2-3) rested after completing creation within six days. They cease working and worship God all day on the seventh day which begins on Friday at sunset and continues to the rising of "three stars" on Saturday night. Jews worship and do religious education at synagogues or wherever they may gather eight believers. The Epistle to the Hebrews refer to the eternal rest of Christians:

> *"As it is, however, there still remains for God's people a rest like God's resting on the seventh day. For those who receive that rest which God promised*

will rest from their own work, just as God rested from his." **Hebrews 4:9-10**

The proper place for worship and prayers for Muslims is the Mosque, known also as Majid, but there is no constraint to worship only at the mosque. Muslims gather for the Friday Salah or Salat to express gratitude and thanksgiving and to adore God. Friday prayers begin shortly after the zenith of the sun in the sky on Fridays. The duration of Friday prayers varies. It is usually from 11:30 AM to 12:30 PM. It usually includes a sermon.

Unlike Jews who worship corporately on Saturdays and Muslims who worship on Fridays, most Christians worship on Sundays. They worship on Sundays because Jesus (God) conquered death and rose from the dead on the first day of the week[xxxi] (Luke 24:1). In a sermon broadcast from Trans World Radio in the Netherland Antilles in the 1950, the preacher said that Sunday is not a day to rest; it is a *day to, "Run as you have never ran before to proclaim the good news that Jesus lives."* Christians meet on the first day of the week for Eucharist or re-enactment of the Sacrifice of Thanksgiving for the life and victory of Jesus Christ over death. They celebrate by singing hymns, reading the Scriptures, exhorting the congregation to greater faith and godly living. They break bread with a shared cup of wine.

The canonical Gospels of Christianity and the Acts of the Apostles tell us that more than 500 disciples saw Jesus between the Sunday of the resurrection and the day he ascended. Christians continue to worship on Sundays, based on the faith-knowledge that Jesus rose from the dead on that day of the week. Emperor Constantine I acquiesced to the wishes of Christians who had been worshipping on the first day of the week, declaring it a public holiday in the year 321 C.E. The Eastern Orthodox Church refers to Easter Sunday as the beginning of the Eighth Day.

Deities are worshipped because they are either adored or feared. Some sociologists suggest that primitive and unenlightened people are more prone to be religious. All people fear the unpredictable forces of nature. Those who are less exposed to the study of the physical sciences are more prone to interpret lightning and thunder as expressions of an angry God that must be placated. Gilbert Keith Chesterton thought otherwise. He said that religious rituals naturally appeal to the primitive and the sophisticated alike. David Fagerberg, in an essay titled "Chesterton on Ritual," said that sophisticated people perceive themselves as religious experts, and worship is a programmed activity for them. He suggested that ordinary people (whatever that means) worship to maintain their sanity.[xxxii] Ordinary people may be more prone to fear the mysterious?

Chesterton also said that one creates morbidity when one destroys mystery--and that ordinary people are always sane, because they have always been mystics. Another interesting thought of Chesterton is that man can understand everything with the help of what he does not understand. He also said that ordinary people, unlike agnostics, "feel free to doubt their gods while simultaneously are free to believe in them." He probably meant ordinary people are more prone to say, "I do not understand" and to contradict themselves without feeling stupid.

Depending on the cultural milieu in which Judaism, Christianity, and Islam developed, their liturgies reflect their incubators, but their similarity is rooted in the sameness of their origin. Former United Nations Secretary General, Kofi Annan suggests that all great religions and traditions overlap on fundamental principles of human conduct and the equality of human beings in the sight of God.[xxxiii] They ought to, because God is their ultimate source. Williams James in *The Varieties of Religious Experience* suggests that religion consists of a belief that there is an unseen order, and that the social good is attained when everyone adjusts to that order.

Institutionalized religion suffered a knock-out punch in May 2004, when the voters in India supported the Congress Party's promised mandate to secularize India.[xxxiv] Institutionalized religion does however rein in the tendency to fracture the socio-religious order.

Although religion and science have coexisted uncomfortable, they have more in common than what divides them. They are both motivated by faith. Erudite scientists who had been formed by religious institutions are oftentimes very self-conflicted. Pierre Teilhard de Chardin felt that to be conscious of the continuation of global evolution is being religious or spiritual. He refers to that condition as the zenith of the evolutionary process.[xxxv] Human beings experience the evolutionary process sporadically; sometimes barely advancing, and other time like a cyclone or hurricane. By this, all people live with the ideal of affirming affinity with God.

To be religious, he said, does not demand that one be irrational. He implied that the religious state is oxymoronic and does require a measure of irrationality. Religious people, including clergy, are mystics. Christian clergy who imitate Jesus of Nazareth become icons of Him--they with Him are the de facto hosts at the Eucharist.

All religious functionaries are mystics. They, like Jesus Christ, reflect to believers the infinite unknowable God. The religious person, in return, confesses that God is the unknown—the beyond which is akin.

6

THE TIMELINE OF ABRAHAMIC RELIGIOUS EMERGENCE

The three Abrahamic religions have a timeline which dates to the 19th century, before the Common Era. The timeline was previously expressed as years "Before (the birth of) Christ" (BC) and years after Christ or "Anno Domini" AD. Because this is a study of the three Abrahamic religions, I choose to use the non-sectarian time-line "B.C.E. (before the Common Era) and C.E (the Common Era), which is used in academia and global trade and commerce.

The Abrahamic Religions date to approximately 1850 B.C.E. when God called Abram, the leader of a clan of 318 men in Ur of the Chaldees (Mesopotamia).and sent him north to Padden-Aram and then south through Palestine into Egypt and back to Palestine. That was less than 400 years after the date that James Ussher, archbishop of the Church of Ireland, proposed as the creation of the earth. Ussher's proposed date of the creation as October 23, 4004 B.C.E. is obviously wrong. The following is the supposed dateline of the Abrahamic religious faiths.

BEFORE THE COMMON ERA

About 1850 B.C.E.	God called (Abram) Abraham and initiated a Covenant relationship with him.
1250 B.C.E.	The exodus from Egypt and the giving and receiving of the Torah at Sinai (Horeb).
1030 B.C.E.	The monarchy established in Israel (King Saul).
950 B.C.E.	The building of the First Temple (Solomon).
931 B.C.E.	Solomon died, and the Kingdom is divided (Rehoboam: Judah, and Jeroboam: Israel/Samaria).
722 B.C.E.	Assyrian captivity of Israel. (References the Ten Lost Northern tribes of Israel).
621 B.C.E.	Restoration and purification of the Temple in Jerusalem by King Josiah.
597 & 586 B.C.E.	Babylonian captivities of Judah and destruction of the (Solomon's) Temple.
539 B.C.E.	Cyrus's conquest of Babylon and his decree that returned exiles in Babylon to their ancestral homelands. Judeans (Jews) returned to Judah.
515-520 B.C.E.	**The building of the second temple.**
20 B.C.E.	Elaborate expansion of the Second Temple by the Idumean-Jewish King Herod.
200 B.C.E.	The Rabbinic Period begins.

THE COMMON ERA

6 B.C.E — **1 C.E. The birth of Jesus**

33-36 C.E. — The crucifixion and resurrection of Jesus (Christ) of Nazareth.

65-70 C.E. — Civil War within Jerusalem. Roman conquest and destruction of the Second Temple.

90-100 C.E. — The canonization of the Jewish Scriptures (Christian O. T. at the Synod of Yamnia.

132-135 C.E. — Bar Kokhbah Rebellion. Rome expelled the Jews from Jerusalem. Jerusalem was renamed Aelia Capitolinia. A pagan Temple was built on the site.

311 C. E. — Emperor Galerius issued an edict of Toleration in the Roman Empire. Religious toleration facilitated freedom of religion for all people.

600 C.E. — The Babylonian Talmud is complete and the Rabbinic Age ends.

614 C.E. — **Persia (Iran) captured Jerusalem and Jews were permitted to return there.**

632 C.E. — The death of Muhammad and the birth of Islam as a religion as well as a political and military force.

1054 C. E. — The Roman Catholic and Eastern Orthodox Churches mutually excommunicated the other with documents placed on the altar at the Cathedral in Constantinople.

1291 C.E.	Egyptian Moslems from Cairo captured Jerusalem and the Mamluk Period began.
1517 C.E.	The Reformation of the Western Church began in Germany. (Martin Luther)
1917 C.E.	The British defeated the Turks and issued the Balfour Declaration: A commitment not to obstruct establishment of a Jewish homeland in Palestine.
1948	Creation of the State of Israel.

7

JUDEO-CHRISTIAN SCRIPTURES AS SALVATION HISTORY

When the Israelites petitioned the judge Samuel to appoint a king to lead them, Samuel told them that God is their King (I Sam. 8:1f). Israel was a theocracy even when Saul and David reigned as their kings. The prophets kept reminding them that God (YHWH) was King of the Covenant Community.

The Scriptures of Judaism is the salvation history of the Jewish people. The New Testament Scriptures and the Jewish Canon of Scriptures are the salvation history of Christianity. The canon of Judaism and the Qur'an is the salvation history of Islam. Those Scriptures document the trajectory of faith communities which believe that God revealed "Self" to them.

God and Moses led a horde of unspecified ethnics from Egypt to Palestine by way of the Sinai desert. That was probably the largest migration of undocumented people in the history of humanity. Referred to only as Hebrews, they were probably foreign ethnics living in Egypt. Many of them were probably Semitic people. They may have included descendants of the "Joseph Clan," which had settled in Northern Egypt in the 18th century B.C.E. Others may have been Anatolians, Greeks, Mediterranean islanders, other Southern Europeans, Mesopotamians, and possibly some Berbers from North Africa. They were identified in archeological documents as "Habiru or Hapiru."

Names looking like Abram (Abraham), Isaac, Jacob, and Joseph have been found at archeological digs throughout the region. The story that Abram and his entourage and their descendants traveled to and from Egypt and spent a long time at an oasis in the Sinai is plausible. The exodus community must have spent a long time at Sinai to develop a covenant community before going on their way to Palestine.

Much of the divine mandate for their new community may have been revealed to other ancient peoples. The Judeo-Christian Scriptures said that they were in the Sinai for 40 years. The revealed laws and liturgy may have been a collection of the history, geography, theology, philosophy, and mythology of the trajectory of all the people in that assembly.

People, including armies and traders, moved between the Mesopotamian and the Egyptian civilizations over many generations. The documents uncovered by archeologists make credible the Judeo-Christian and Muslim salvation history. Their Scriptures are not legends. They are faith knowledge. Jews, Christians, and Muslims believe that (YHWH) always hears the cry of the oppressed and delivers them. Their stories are history and theologies of liberation.

The section of the Jewish people's salvation history in which Moses led them from Egypt to Sinai is the most dramatic episode of any known salvation history. Many of them were successful immigrants in Egypt before a regime change. They may have been the Hyksos, "ruler of foreign lands" and may have ruled in upper Egypt from about 1630 to 1521 B.C.E. They may have included descendants of the "Jacob and Joseph" clan, and some Berbers from North Africa. They may have been the people referred to in some archeological documents as "Hapiru or Habiru."

Moses and his brother Aaron (Exodus 18 - 20) responded to the call of God as did Abraham. The Hebrew people as they were called going out of Egypt, comprised a confederation of clans. They became the nations of Israel and Judah. The name change happened (Gen. 32:28) when Jacob, the grandson of Abraham and the father of Joseph, had an epiphany which changed the trajectory of his life and the life of the Hebrews. On his way back to Canaan from Paddan-Aram to make peace with his brother Esau who had been defrauded of his birthright, he wrestled all night with an angel (man) on the bank of the Jabbok river. Jacob prevailed against the man and demanded that the angel (man) bless him as a condition of letting go of him. The blessing came with a name change, "You will be called Israel" which means, "You have prevailed against God."

There isn't any documentation of the enslavement of the ancestors of the Israelites in the annals of Egypt. The only record of that slavery in Egypt is that recorded in the Hebrew Bible (Old Testament). Is the story fact or fiction? It may be a combination of both. There may have been slavery in Egypt at or after the 16th Dynasty.

History is often ambiguous. A foreign group of Semitic and Asians ruled much of Egypt as the 15th and 16th dynasties. Known as "Hyksos", Herodotus may have erred when he named them the "Shepherd Kings or Desert Princes." They were foreigners in Egypt and may have been overthrown by an ethnic Egyptian dynasty at about 1632 B.C.E. From the Nile delta where they had settled, they sacked the old capital at Memphis. This dynasty was renowned for their innovation. They employed new military technology, added new types of daggers, scimitars, horses and chariots, and composite bow and arrows. They employed bronze weapons, used pottery, weaved on looms, had new musical instruments and styles of music, and engaged in advanced animal husbandry and agronomy. Pharaoh Sheshi ruled from the new capital at Avaris.

When the Hyksos were firmly established in the north, a new line of native rulers emerged in the southern region around Thebes and soon controlled Elephantine and Abydos in the middle of the country. They sustained an uneasy truce with the Hyksos until they felt strong enough to attack. They did so under Pharaoh Tao II, which began the 17th Dynasty. Despite the scientific advances, there were challenges that overwhelmed the military and political resources of the Hyksos.

Pharaoh Tao and his elder son died fighting the Hyksos, and Ahmose, a younger son succeeded him as the pharaoh. That was probably the beginning of the enslavement of the foreign (Hebrew) peoples. The date was probably 1550 B.C.E. That may explain the Biblical reference (Exodus 1:8), "The new pharaoh who did not know Joseph." The foreign policy and economic progress of the 17th and subsequent dynasties suggests a socio-political and economic revolution.

Sigmund Freud suggested that Jewish monotheism is modeled on the monotheism of Amenhotep IV (d.1292 B.C.E). He theorized that Moses may have been greatly influenced by Amenhotep. Amenhotep IV (Akhenaten) and his queen, Nefertiti, initiated a radical break from the polytheistic Egyptian pantheon and its Atum priesthood. The socio-political unrest generated by the religious disconnect of Amenhotep (Akhenaten) and the Atum priests weakened the body politic. Moses, or someone who answered to his description, mobilized the Hebrews and led them out of Egypt to Sinai (Horeb). The Hebrews may have been the Hyksos and their supporters. They had an epiphany at Sinai, and YHWH spoke with Moses from a burning bush (Gen. 3:2-10).

The theory of Sigmund Freud that links Moses and Akhenaten should not be ignored. Ahmed Osman, in the preface of his book, *Moses and Akhenaten*, theorized that Moses may not have been a Hebrew and even that Akhenaten and Moses are the same person. Interestingly, the lineage of Pharaoh Amenhotep was expunged from the list of kings because of his supposed monotheistic heresy.

Regardless of the identity of Moses, he was probably a member of the pharaoh's household as a youth. According to the Scriptures of Judaism, he was a foster-grandson of a pharaoh and probably served as an officer in the Egyptian armed forces. He obviously knew all the routes out of

Egypt. He reportedly led close to 600,000 Hebrews out of Egypt. That must have been a formidable operation, which he accomplished successfully by evading Egyptian army patrols. He had multiple epiphanies in the desert at Sinai. The most dramatic were the bush fire that did not scorch the bush. A voice from the burning bush identified itself as, "I am who I am (YHWH)". It suggests that God is dynamic and continuously revealing. God is the, "I am who I am" and also, "I am who I shall be." The law code was also revealed to Moses for Israel.

YHWH commissioned Moses to lead the Hebrews from Egypt into the land that God had prepared for them to settle. He was like another Abraham. He became their supreme leader under YHWH and developed a confederation of clans from the horde of loose foreign ethnics. That group became a theocratic community.

8

GOD IS THE ONE GREAT MYSTERY

Saul of Tarsus was a Pharisee and rabbi who was initially highly motivated to crush the aspiration of the disciples of Jesus of Nazareth to proclaim his resurrection and divinity. His opposition to the nascent Christian faith abruptly ended when he had a mysterious encounter (Acts 9:3f). Saul the rabbi became Paul the Christian evangelist and theologian. Seeing an altar to the "Unknown God" on Mars Hill in the Grecian city of Athens, Paul embraced the opportunity to proclaim that Jesus Christ is that "Unknown God:

PAUL'S SERMON ON MARS HILL

And Paul stood up in the midst of the Areopagus and said, 'Men of Athens, I observe that you are very religious in all respects. For while I was passing through and examining the objects of your worship, I also found an altar with this inscription, "To an unknown God." What therefore you worship

> *in ignorance, this I proclaim to you. The God who made the world and all things in it, since He is Lord of heaven and earth, does not dwell in temples made with hands; neither is he served by human hands, as though He needed anything, since He Himself gives to all life and breath and all things; and He made from one, every nation of mankind to live on all the face of the earth, having determined their appointed times, and the boundaries of their habitation, . . . For we also are His off-springs. . . He has fixed a day in which He will judge the world in righteousness through a Man whom He has appointed, having furnished proof to all men by raising Him from the dead.*[xxxvi]

This philosophical discourse of Paul did not apparently win many converts to Christianity. Proclamations win converts. This may explain why there isn't an epistle of Paul to the Athenians.

JUDAISM

Judaism is the religion and culture of the Jewish people. It was initiated in the 12th century B.C.E., when God called Moses from within a burning bush in the Sinai and commissioned him to go and tell the Pharaoh in Egypt to free the foreign peoples who had been living in slavery. The pharaoh capitulated after a prolonged verbal struggle and the unleashing of the power of God against Egypt. The pharaoh capitulated and the Hebrews, probably as many as 600,000, followed Moses across the Red (Reed) Sea into the Sinai, where God promised to protect them conditionally in their ongoing journey to the land promised to them. That Exodus from Egypt is the single most important religious and political liberation in history.

The significance of their stopover in the Sinai cannot be overestimated. The Hebrews who were later known as Israel and Jews, formed a religious and political community in the Sinai. The community teaches that God gave them the Torah, a law code to guide them. The Torah has 613 commands. Those laws are summarized in the Decalogue (Exodus 20:2-17). Guided by the Torah, the Israelites became a religious community with One God and a set of religious and social mores. The laws of biblical Israel are an example of the fact that history is often cyclical, and that God does not operate in a vacuum.[xxxvii] God may have revealed much of that law code to King Hammurabi and the people of Babylon nearly 800 years earlier.

While there is no documentation of the enslavement of the Israelites in the annals of Egyptian history-- not at all surprising, because histories are written by victors and historians describe themselves positively. The Book of Exodus reports the events as follows:

> *"A new king arose over Egypt, who did not know Joseph. And he said to his people, 'Behold, the people of the sons of Israel are more and mightier than we. Now let us deal wisely with them, lest they multiply and in the event of war, they also join themselves to those who hate us . . ."* - **Exodus 1:8-10 (KJAV)**

Jewish sectarians run the gamut of ultra-orthodox to liberal. Some orthodox Jews manifest their faith as Fundamentalist Sectarians, some of whom are painstakingly xenophobic. Reformed Jews work for rapport with non-Jewish peoples. Liberal Jews cite their foci of Judaism as: Israel and the Jewish Diaspora. Liberal Judaism pledges to work with all people, including the protagonists of conflicts in the Middle East, to eradicate ignorance and build bridges of understanding for the establishment of peace on the earth.[xxxviii] Jewish Orthodox Fundamentalists advocate an advanced form of xenophobia and the restoration of the Davidic Monarchy, dispense with democracy, promotion of violence against opponents, and sidelining of non-Jewish residents in Israel.[xxxix] They painstakingly catalog their past suffering as a religious community, especially the sufferings meted out to them by despots in the Middle East and Europe. Jews list Christians among their oppressors. Christians accuse them of killing Jesus of Nazareth, known also as Jesus Christ.

Faithfulness to the Torah is a dogma of Judaism. The Torah is more than a book of laws. It is a guide book to build and maintain the covenant community and cult of Judaism. The Torah may be a composite document which corresponds to the experiences of the Hebrews (Jews). It may be compiled of extracts from law codes, such as the Code of King Hammurabi of Mesopotamia. That code has 282 laws.[xl] Until Rome destroyed the Second Temple in Jerusalem, Jews practiced animal sacrifice to atone for their communal as well as personal sins.

YHWH withheld divine protection from Israel whenever it breeched the terms of the covenant. Punishment is meted out variably as natural disasters, attacks from neighboring nations, and sometimes exile to adversarial nations like Assyria and Babylon, notably in 722 B.C.E. and 697 B.C.E., respectively. The people of Judah and Israel believed that YHWH enabled and guided Cyrus, the Persian Emperor, to issue the decree of toleration which enabled the repatriation of the Jews to Judah.

The Judeans who returned to Judah under the leadership of Ezra and Nehemiah had two distinct ideologies. They were:

i. The Ezra School which was Particularistic.[xli]

ii. The Deuteronomic School which was universalistic.

The Ezra School prevailed as **Judaism.** The religion of Judaism was so named because it was the religious cult of Judah. The pre-exile Judeans had a well-defined understanding of nationalism and monotheism. Although the exile had a negative effect on nationalism and the cult,[xlii] many Judean exiles in Babylon participated actively in synagogue activities and ceremonies. They studied the Torah, maintained ethnic and religious purity, did sabbath observances, practiced circumcision, celebrated feasts, and observed Jewish rituals and ceremonials.[xliii] Ezra guided the returnees to renovate the Temple, to study the Torah, and to reestablish their identity as Jews. He also imposed orthodoxy on the people who had remained in Judah and Israel at the time of the exile.

Maimonides (d. 1204 C. E.) supported that orthodoxy. Citing the Book of Deuteronomy (6:4) *"Hear O Israel, the Lord is our God, the Lord is one,"* he said, *"If a man claims to be God, he is a liar."* He went on to say, *"God is unity unlike any other unity."* Given that thinking, he rejected Christianity.

Jewish orthodoxy came up against many challenges which made the rabbis reluctant to allow a commentary on the Torah. The continued development of the Mishnah greatly concerned Orthodox and Conservative rabbis. While the Orthodox and Conservative rabbis fought the development of the Mishnah, other rabbis began expanding the Gemara. The Gemara is a commentary on the Mishnah.

When a fierce Zoroastrian sect seized power in Persia in the sixth century, and lawlessness spread across the region, even into the Roman Empire, the rabbis who constituted a collective magisterium felt that the murder of Jewish scholars threatened the repository of Jewish knowledge. They began to support codification of the Mishnah and Gemara.[xliv] The threat to Judaism by the Zoroastrians enabled the codification of the Mishna that Rabbi Judah's (the Prince) had prepared. That development is one of many that show Judaism to be a dynamic faith that is always evolving in theory and practice.[xlv] Jesus of Nazareth was among the rabbis that believe in an evolving Judaism. He was addressed on several occasions as "Rabbi," and He taught a band of disciples unmolested by the Jewish authorities over a period of about three years. He even apparently read a Scripture in a synagogue. They were impressed with the eloquence of His exposition but were greatly offended when He challenged their xenophobia (Luke 4:24-28).

Judaism never existed in a vacuum. Despite the commitment to battle religious syncretism, many rabbis cultivated personal relationship with the Greco-Roman colonial administrators. The powerful rabbi, Judah the Prince, apparently cultivated the favor of the emperors Antoninus Pius (138-161 C.E.) and Marcus Aurelius (161-180 C.E.). His greatness and prominence may be attributed to his willing complicity with whatever was the contemporary trend.

Rome astutely knit together the diverse ethnics to build a powerful Empire. The Roman Senate appointed

Herod, an Idumean-Jewish ethnic known also as Herod the Great, as the King of Judah in the year 37 B.C.E. Orthodox Judeans were disappointed with the appointment, and some felt that his appointment was the venting of YHWH's displeasure for their continuing apostasy. Although there was resistance to Herod's appointment as king, he surprised them when he rebuilt the Temple in grand proportions and style and became a bridge between the diverse ethnicity of his kingdom. An Avant Gard rabbi like Jesus was not easily embraced in that tense socio-political and religious context. Many opposed His anti-establishment messages and actions.

The Roman Army destroyed the Temple in 70 C.E. after about five years of Jewish rebellion against Rome and Jewish internecine riots within Jerusalem. The city remained in ruins and gangs developed amidst the city's ruins. Bar Kokhbah tapped into the frustration of people living in and around Jerusalem. He raised an army of discontents for his anti-Rome revolution in 132 C.E. Rome retaliated by levelling Jerusalem in 135 C.E. and building a temple to Jupiter Capitolinus on the Temple mount. Rome renamed Jerusalem Aelia Capitolinia.[xlvi] Rebels at Masada held out in hard to reach caves on the hill around the Dead Sea. That further infuriated the Romans. The loss of the land and the Temple took away two very important political and religious anchors from the Jews and Judaism. Jerusalem, Aelia Capitolinia after 135 C.E., had become a neglected region of the Roman Empire with scant security. Arab Muslims led by Caliph Umar ibn Al-Khattab took it from Rome in 638 C.E.

The Scriptures of Judaism was canonized in 90 C.E. at the Synod of Yamnia, a city on the Mediterranean Coast. It comprised 22 scrolls, which became the 39 books of the Judeo-Christian Old Testament. A criterion for canonicity was that the scrolls be written within the lifetime of Moses through that of Artaxerxes--probably Artaxerxes I, the fifth king of Persia (465-424 B.C.E.). Another standard of orthodoxy was that the texts be free of Hellenizing or Greek philosophical ideas.

Great kings of Israel and Judah were identified by their faithfulness to the Torah. Kings Uzziah, Hezekiah, and Josiah were good kings. Manasseh, Amon, and Jehoiachin were bad kings because they allowed idolatry, which was national "adultery." According to Maimonides, Jews classify Jesus of Nazareth and Bar Kockbah together as the most damaging of all the "false messiahs." He rejected the notion that Jesus was the Messiah of Judaism. Maimonides' Orthodox Judaism rejected what Jesus taught as heresy.

The title "Messiah" was ambiguous, and many Judeans were proclaiming themselves messiah during the first century B.C.E. and the first century C.E. Everyone who was anointed to an office was a messiah. That included priests and kings. David said of Saul, "*God forbid that I should touch the Lord's anointed.*" (I Sam. 26:11; II Sam. 23:1; Is. 45:1; Ps. 20:6; KJAV) It is understandable, given the many claimant to the title "Messiah" that the High priests and their Sanhedrin put the spotlight on every claimant. Judaism is still waiting for the Messiah to come. The messianic fulfillment of Israel is conditional on, among other things:

i. *The building of the Third Temple during the lifetime of the Messiah (Isaiah 2:2-3; 56:6-7; 60: 7; Ezek. 37:26-27; Malachi 3:4).*

ii. *The return home of most of the Jewish people that went into exile (Deut. 30:3; Is. 11:11-12; Jer. 30:3; 32:37; Ezek. 11:17; 36:24).*

iii. *The ushering in of an age of universal peace. (Hosea 2:20; Micah 4:1-4; No more war or preparation for war (Isa. 2:4).*

iv. *The Messiah would preside over the proclamation that brings the universal knowledge of God that unites all peoples on the earth (Zech. 3:9; 8:23; 14:9, 16; Isaiah 45:23; 66:23; Jer. 31:32; Ezek. 38: 23; Zeph. 3:9; Psalm 86:9).*

v. *All people would experience, and embrace, and observe Torah celebrations (Deut. 30:8, 10; Jer. 31:32; Ezek. 11:19-20; 36:26-27; 37:24).*

vi. *The Messiah would be from the Tribe of Judah and a direct descendant of King David through paternal genealogy (Gen. 49:10). The prophet Ezekiel sketched a great word portrait of the Messiah of Judaism (Ezekiel 37:24–28).*

Many Judeans in Babylon opted to remain when Cyrus guaranteed them safety to repatriate to Judah under the leadership of Nehemiah and Ezra. They had become economic and social successes in Babylon. The post-exilic religious Jews believed that the Messiah of Israel's expectation would restore the grandeur and military might of the Davidic dynasty. He should satisfy all the conditions of the Messiah as prophesied by Isaiah (11:1-9), Jeremiah (25:5-6; 30:7-10; 33:14-16), Ezekiel (34:11-31; 37:21-28), and Hosea (3:4-5). He would be the greatest prophet in history, and would be second only to Moses to whom God gave the Torah. The did not believed Jesus satisfied that expectation.

Rabbi Judah Halevi and Maimonides suggested that Jesus and Muhammad may have been reformers who were preparing an ethical Jewish Monotheism. Maimonides, an Orthodox Jew, contrast ethical monotheism and religious monotheism. Maimonides may have been referring to Jesus ironically as an ethical reformer rather than a religious leader. Orthodox rabbi Jacob Emden and Reformed rabbi Moses Mendelssohn opined that the teaching of Jesus of history may have been closer to Judaism than either the text of the Christian Canonical Gospels and Jewish history indicates. That insight questions the credibility of both the rabbinic and the Christian historians.

Jews for Jesus, an organization founded by Moishe Rosen in 1973, which was at one time believed to be a reformed branch of Judaism, has been discredited by Jewish as well as mainstream Christian denominations. The Task Force on Missionaries and Cults of the Jewish Community Relations Council of New York, which comprises the four major Jewish sects, issued the following statement on "Jews for Jesus" in 1993:

> *"On several occasions leaders of the four major Jewish movements have signed on to joint statements opposing Hebrew-Christian theology*

and tactics. In part they said: 'Though Hebrew Christianity claims to be a form of Judaism, it is not . . . it deceptively uses the sacred symbols of Jewish observance . . . as a cover to convert Jews to Christianity, a belief system that is antithetical to Judaism . . . Hebrew Christians are in radical conflict with the communal interests and the destiny of the Jewish people. They have crossed an unbridgeable chasm by accepting another religion."[xlvii]

9

JUDAISM: COULD JESUS OF NAZARETH BE THE SON OF GOD?

Jews reject the notion that God can become human or that God can procreate with a human being. They therefore refused to listen the philosophical arguments put forth by Christian incarnational theologians. The English word messiah is from "Mashiach" the transliteration of a Hebrew word. It is also translated as Christ and the anointed one. Israel supposed that the Messiah would be an aristocrat. A Messiah may be a king or a high priest. The prophet Isaiah (Is. 45:1-12) named King Cyrus of Persia a messiah, because he repatriated the Judaeans and the Israelites from exile in Babylon and facilitated the rebuilding of the Temple in Jerusalem. King Cyrus is the only non-Jew that is recognized as a messiah by the Jews.

Judaism debunks Christian messianism on two principal counts. The first is the ethical concern about the co-mixing of the human and the divine. The other is that the genealogy of Jesus in the Gospels according to

Matthew and Luke contradicts even that which Christianity teaches about Jesus as Messiah. The Gospels according to Matthew and Luke trace the genealogy of Jesus of Nazareth though Joseph to Abraham and through Joseph to Adam, respectively. If the conception of Jesus of Nazareth was a de facto gestation of the Spirit of God, the genealogy ought to be through Mary and not Joseph. Neither genealogy in the above referenced Gospels traced the nativity through Mary. The Matthean genealogy reads:

> *"From . . . exile in Babylon to the birth of Jesus, the following ancestors are listed: Jehoiachin, Shealtiel, Zadok, Achim, Eliud, Eleazar, Matthan, Jacob, and Joseph, who was the husband of Mary, of whom Jesus was born."* **Matthew 1:12-16 (GNB-TEV).**

According to Matthew (1:20-21), Mary was pregnant and she knew that she was still a virgin. An angel visited Joseph, to whom Mary was engaged to be married, and assured him that the child in Mary's womb was immaculately conceived of the Holy Spirit.

The Matthean genealogy ironically put Joseph in the lineage of Jeconiah (Jehoiakim) (Matt. 1:11; Jer. 22:24). The religious reason given for Judah's exile was the idolatry of her kings. Jehoiakim (Jeconiah) went as a Judean exiled to Babylon in 587-6 B.C.E. and his ancestry lost the inheritance to the throne of David (Jer. 22:28-30; 36:30, & 31).

Jesus' Jewishness is established through his mother. That satisfies the tradition of Judaism. Lineage is matrilineal. Joseph is not necessary to the nativity of Jesus Christ. Given that his patrilineality is morally tainted, his connection to Jesus is a distraction. He is at best a consort or security companion of Mary.

GOD EMPTIED "SELF" INTO A MAN

10

IS JESUS A JEWISH PROPHET AND/OR A ZEALOT?

Judaism has a prescribed period or chronology of prophecy. That began about the year 750 B.C.E. and ended at about the year 450 B.C.E. It began with Isaiah and ended with the deaths of Haggai, Zechariah, and Malachi. That is about 450 years before the birth of Jesus of Nazareth. The rabbis may have designated that narrow timeframe as the age of prophecy to delegitimize anti-establishment zealots who spoke truth to power in the Hasmoneans through to the Roman era.

The rabbis said that the zealots who referred to him during the procession into Jerusalem as, "*The prophet Jesus, from Nazareth in Galilee*" (Matt. 21:11, TEV), were misinformed and deluded. The rabbis citing the demand of the urban rabble to "Crucify Him" a few days later at his trial, suggest that they rather than uncultivated Galileans, understood that Jesus was one of a series of zealots.

The word zealot was not always a negative appellation in the annals of Jewish history. The historian Josephus said that zealots were radical defenders of the Covenant and constituted the fourth sect of Judaic society. They were perceived positively as divinely sanctioned radicals who put their lives on the line to defend the Torah and Israel against threats to the orthodoxy of the faith. They had an enviable place in the formative period of Judaism and Israel as a nation. Some of Jesus' disciples may have been zealots who zealously guarded the Temple and harassed Roman soldiers who they felt were defiling their land.

When some Samaritans killed some Jews along the road from Jerusalem to Galilee and procurator Cumanus hesitated to seek out and punish the killers, Jewish zealots made an incursion into the Samaritan neighborhood of Acrabatene toparchy and "indiscriminately murdered everyone they came across and burned a number of villages."[xlviii] Such radical behavior and citizen justice ought to be discouraged, but it was applauded by many contemporary Jews. The Jews that were against Jesus were not associating him with Jewish nationalism. They were fixated on identifying him as secular criminal zealot destabilizers of civil society.

The Essenes, a monastic sect of Judaism and contemporaries of the Jesus of history, had some prophets among them. Their hope and aspiration for Israel, Judah, and of Judaism were more spiritual than that of their contemporary Sadducees, Pharisees, and Zealots. Jesus may have been identified as a pacifist. A letter written in Hebrew and apparently from Bar Kockbah to one of his captains, was found in a cave at Qumran when the Ecole Biblique took over the continuing search for the Dead Sea scrolls in 1951. It suggests that the Galilean followers of Jesus were not supportive of the Revolution because Jesus had said, "*My Kingdom is not of this world.*"[xlix]

D. S. Russell tells us that several Essenes were able to foretell the future by their reading of the sacred texts.[l] Jesus was among those prophets. He was more a prophet than a zealot. Like the Essenes He read the signs of the time and told what is coming. While on the Mount of Olives, He told his disciples;

> *"See that you are not troubled; for all these things must come to pass, but the end is not yet. For nations will rise against nation, and kingdom against kingdom, and there will be famines."*
> **Matthew 24:6f (KJAV)**

He may have been a prophet, but Judaism denied him accreditation as a Jewish prophet. Some of His disciples may have been attracted to Him because they believed He was leading a zealot's band. He critiqued Pharisee and Sadducees alike in his prophetic teaching and frustrated the radical political aspirations of some zealots. Judas Iscariot was obviously frustrated, because Jesus was posturing more like an Essene than as a Jewish Messiah. Bruce Chilton[li] concurred with Josephus that Jesus was a Talmid obsessed with purity and was not a zealot.

Jesus probably knew the Essenes' Teacher of Righteousness and may have been a Teacher of Righteousness. He may not himself fully exemplify the monastic vision and lifestyle of the Essenes, but He could have been an associate member of the Essenes. His critique of contemporary Judaism and support for reforms made Him a target of persecution by the High Priest and the Sanhedrin.

He probably attracted several of the socially uncultivated Galileans and many disaffected and alienated urban proletariats in Jerusalem and adjacent towns. The Jerusalem-based Levites and Pharisaic contemporaries of Jesus felt that Galileans were renegades and social misfits in Jerusalem society. The Temple priests required an elaborate ritual cleansing before giving them access to the Temple. The Essenes felt that the requisite public cleansing ritual for Galileans was superfluous because God had already cleansed Israel. The simple baptism of John the Baptist in the Jordan River was probably done to protest the elaborate public cleansing mandated by the priests for the Galileans.

The jubilant crowd that followed Jesus into Jerusalem were the social and religious disillusioned masses who were looking for a leader to protect the Torah and restore the sanctity of the Temple. They reflect his folk-hero status popularity among Galileans. They believed that He was a reformer of Judaism. They saw qualities akin to that of Phinehas.

> **Numbers 25:11; 31:6 (KJAV):**
> *"And the Lord said to Moses, 'Phinehas, the son of Eleazar, son of Aaron the priest has turned back my wrath from the people of Israel in my jealousy."*

It is obvious that the Jesus of history from Nazareth was a complex person. He had the zeal of the zealots, the passion for peace of the Essenes, and a flare for prophetic utterances.

GOD EMPTIED "SELF" INTO A MAN

11

JEWISH MONOTHEISM AND CHRISTIAN TRINITARIANISM

The first commandment or the first statement of the Decalogue in the Torah of Judaism (Exodus 20:3) is the mandate that the Hebrew people commit themselves absolutely to One God. It reads:

> *"You shall have no other gods before me . . ..*
> *You shall not make for yourself a graven image, or*
> *any likeness of anything that is in heaven above, or*
> *that is in the earth beneath . . ."*
> **Exodus 20:3-4 (RSV)**

Judaism mandates monotheism without icons. It is a compelling mandate because it is attributed to God (YHWH). God called the Hebrew horde into a covenant relationship with the unknown mystery while they camped at Sinai. The name of the unknown mystery was revealed to Moses as, "I AM WHO I AM" (Exod. 19:1-13). It is unlike any other religious dogma. God is not identified by a name or any indication of ethnicity or sex but as, "I am who I am," or "I am who you will find me to be." The one God of Judaism cannot be replicated. The God of Judaism is an apparent idea; "I am who I am" or "I am who you will find me to be."

Moses, Aaron, and the cult of "I am who I am" named the divine apparition "YHWH." Although YHWH is one, there were other names for God than YHWH or Jehovah. The name Baal was almost totally eradicated with the destruction of the Canaanites civilization, but the name El survived as the name Elohim which was at times use interchangeably with YHWH. The kingdom of Israel divided when Solomon died, and Jeroboam who reigned over the 10 tribes in the north and wanted a total break from the Solomonic dynasty of Rehoboam and the Temple cult in Jerusalem, set up cults of idolatry. Judah in the south remained faithful to YHWH. God was known later in Israel-Judah as "YHWH-Elohim."[lii] YHWH-Elohim is probably the one God.

The Judeo-Christian Bible suggests that YHWH-Elohim presides over a pantheon and allows all people the freedom to select their god. The Hebrews were however predestined to be YHWH-Elohim's people and to worship only YHWH-Elohim.

The Book of the Psalms reads:

"God presides in the heavenly council; in the assembly of the gods, he gives his decisions."
Psalm 82:1 (TEV)

> *"For the Lord is a mighty God, a mighty king above all the gods."* **Psalm 95:3 (TEV)**

> *"No one in heaven is like you Lord, none of the heavenly beings is your equal. You are feared in the council of the holy ones; they all stand in awe of you."* **Psalms 89:6-7 (TEV)**

The Book of Deuteronomy said that YHWH assigns people and gods to wherever He wills:

> *"The Most-High assigned nations their lands: he determined where peoples should live. He assigned to each nation a heavenly being, but Jacob's descendants he chose for Himself."* **Deuteronomy 32:8-9 (TEV)**

The people of Israel are cognizant of YHWH's power and commitment to them.

> *"No other nation, no matter how great, has a god who is so near when they need Him as the Lord our God is to us."* **Deuteronomy 4:7 (TEV)**

In a dialogue between Pinchas Lapide and Jurgen Moltmann, a Jewish and a Christian theologian respectively, Lapide cited F. C. Conybeare, who in 1901 said that the Trinitarian statement is absent from all three of Eusebius' pre-Nicaean copies of the Gospel according to St. Matthew. [liii] That is an important observation. Many Christians, including those who confess the Trinitarian Doctrine, are strict monotheists. Some Christians argue that there are hints of Trinitarianism in the Judeo-Christian Old Testament. The argument is that trinitarianism does not suggest belief in three gods but acceptance of the fact that God is manifested in more than a single and simple way. Abraham knew God as the One who led out from Ur of Chaldea; his son Isaac knew God as the One who saved him from his father's knife on Mount Moriah; and Jacob knew God as the angel with whom he wrestled and overcame him and got a blessing.[liv] The patriarchs experienced the One Creator God differently. Jews dismiss the arguments that support Trinitarianism as philological gibberish.

Judaism does not deny that God is omnipotent, and that God is "That than which none can be greater, some rabbis see a difference in the Liturgical and the Systematic theology of even great Church fathers such as St. Basil of Caesarea. Basil was pro-Nicaean and probably would defend the mandates of the first Seven Ecumenical Councils, but his prayer[lv] in the Divine Liturgy teeters on the edge of Tritheism. It reads,

> *"O God and Master, Christ, thou king of ages and Maker of all, among all these good things ... For thou art the bread of life, the well of holiness ... together with the Father and the Holy Ghost, now and forever."*

12

PERSPECTIVE OF JUDAISM: WAS THERE A HISTORICAL JESUS (CHRIST) OF NAZARETH?

Josephus who spent about three years as an associate Essene, implied a connection of Jesus to the Essenes. The sect, like Jesus, emphasized purity in preparation for the age to come. Richard Carrier suggests that the religious practices of the Essenes may have been a syncretism of Judaism and Greek mystery religions. They had an elaborate initiation ceremony, which included baptism, a communal meal, swearing to keep the secrets, and believing in personal salvation and resurrection from the dead. Carrier said such mysteries existed in many pre-Christian sects of Judaism,[lvi] and that Jesus of Nazareth exemplifies much of those characteristics.

Sorbonne Professor A. Dupont-Somers compared the teachings of the Essenes and the teachings of Jesus of Nazareth and made the following comment:[lvii]

> *"The Galilean Master as he is presented to us in the writings of the New Testament appears in many respects as an astonishing reincarnation of the Teacher of Righteousness. Like the latter, he preached penitence, poverty, humility, love of one's neighbor, chastity... Like him, he was the Elect and the Messiah of God, the Messiah Redeemer of the world. Like him, he was the object of the hostility of the priests... He found a Church whose adherents fervently awaited His Glorious return."*

Carrier suggested that the death and resurrection of deities were not unique in the context of Greco-Roman and Jewish societies, and he even suggested that references to Jesus in the Antiquities of Josephus may have been interpolations. Carrier's special interest as a scholar is ancient history and not religion. Given that interest and scholarly specialty, he felt that a story on the trial and the death sentence meted out to James, the brother of Jesus, for unspecified charges by the High Priest Ananus may be authentic, given the detailed knowledge of the family of Jesus shown by the high priest.[lviii] Carrier could be wrong, because the death penalty was the prerogative of the Roman court.

Josephus seemed disappointed with the narrators of the life and ministry of Jesus in the Canonical Gospels. He felt that the narrative of the Canonical Gospels was oriented to spirituality and lacked the historical accuracy of Pliny the Younger. He felt that Pliny the Younger wrote as if he knew his uncle, Pliny the Elder. The explanation given for the difference of Pliny's writing style and that of the Christian evangelists is that Pliny was a bureaucrat and bureaucratic correspondence has its peculiar culture.

He notes that although Paul refers to Jesus more than three hundred times in his epistles including the crucifixion (fifteen times) and resurrection (more than thirty times), he never connected the Jesus of faith and the human Jesus.[lix] Paul (Saul) was not a disciple of the Jesus of history. He met Jesus initially as a prosecutor at the trial of Stephen the deacon. And the finale of his conversion was after a mystical meeting with the Jesus Christ of faith.

The verification of the historicity of a person or an event that goes back 2,000 years into antiquity may be determined on faith knowledge only. The evangelists that wrote the Gospels of Jesus of Nazareth wrote their stories more than 30 years after Jesus died and after the stories had passed through many oral versions. The Gospels and the Acts of the Apostles are a mix of history and commentaries.

Richard Carrier sites Radcliffe Edmonds to suggests that myth "consists of factually untrue stories that are historically improbable but symbolically meaningful."[lx] When a person asks whether the story of Jesus Christ is fact of fiction, he/she ought to ask whether the writer genuinely believes he was writing history. If the intention is to write a story which is authentic, the story is authentic faith history.

The intensity of the drama at the initial stage of the development of the Christian Church probably generated much myth. The procession of Jesus into Jerusalem, which precipitated his arrest, trial, and crucifixion, was a norm at that time. Many messianic pretenders probably walked that path. It is, therefore, probably historical.

The ecstatic reaction of the women who saw the empty tomb early that Sunday morning is normal, even if it was unusual for women without familial male companions to go off the beaten tracks into a cemetery under the shadow of darkness. The unusualness of the women at the tomb before daylight is an additional fact which points to verity. It is an unusual detail. That the evangelists said that the women did something unconditional by going to the tomb when they did without father, brother, or uncle was probably factual. The hysterics of the female disciples is a normal reaction to an unusual experience. There intense display of raw emotions at the empty tomb is normal.

Given the speculation that Jesus was probably associated with the Essenes, one wonders why the Essenes were not more visible with Jesus and his disciples. Despite this obvious absence of the Essenes at post-resurrection scenes, scholars still maintain his connection to the Essenes.

Spanish scholar Jose O'Callaghan identified the words "Gennesaret" and "beget" in a scroll and in the Gospel according to Mark (6:52–53) and suggested that the Gospel according to Mark and the scrolls may have influenced each other. The historical Jesus may have been parodied in some scrolls as the reincarnate Teacher of Righteousness. The Teacher of Righteousness and Jesus of Nazareth died in 63 B.C.E. and 30-33 C.E., respectively.

Professor Robert Eisenman, a scholar of Middle-Eastern Religions at California State University, found the word "Messiah" in a fragment of a scroll he studied. He believes that the correlation of the text of a New Testament Gospel and a scroll may suggest liturgical veneration of Jesus as Messiah by the Essenes at Qumran. According to Josephus, the various sects of Judaism did not always acknowledge the others as authentic Judaism.

Jesus was in the process of reforming Judaism. His reform ideals concern Sabbath observance (Matt. 12:1-4), marriage and divorce (19:1-9), and ritual purity (15:1-20). He taught that faithfulness to the Torah was more than repeating formulae and doing ceremonials. It was one's relationship with God. He may have died before He develop an effective teaching, but organized a community and left behind a leadership team of twelve well-trained disciples.

A Jewish sect that lived and worked east of the Roman Empire wrote an anti-Christian propaganda. The writers may have been Babylonian rabbis. They identified Jesus of Nazareth as a criminal, "*Condemned for immorality, sorcery and worshipping idols, and eventually executed because he practiced magic and led Israel astray.*"[lxi] They said that Jesus went into Alexandria, Egypt, when King Jannaeus was killing Jewish rabbis. It counters the version in the Gospel according to Matthew that his mother and Joseph took him as an infant to Egypt to escape Herod's slaughter of the innocents (Matt. 2:13-17). That same Jewish anti-Christian polemic alleged that Jesus was the son of Pandera, a Roman soldier. They maliciously punned "Ben Pandera", son of Pandera, instead of "ben Parthenos," son of a virgin.[lxii] Such negative polemic and critique are more likely to be directed to actual historical characters than to mythological ones.

GOD EMPTIED "SELF" INTO A MAN

CHRISTIANITY

Christianity is a monotheistic religion. It believes and worships one God. It teaches that the God of Abram (Abraham), Isaac, and Jacob was revealed to Moses as YHWH, and gave Moses a code of law. It also believes and teaches that God became a human being--the male child of the Virgin Mary. That child was conceived without a human father and gestated naturally in the womb of the young virgin who was a descendant of the Jewish patriarch Abraham through Isaac, Jacob, and King David. Given that historical trajectory, Christianity shares a common religious lineage with Judaism and latterly Islam. Most Christians believe that God satisfies all human needs and is manifested as Father, Son, and Holy Ghost (Holy Spirit). Trinitarianism is explained as the Christian's understanding of the providence of God, and on the commission written in the canonical Gospel according to Matthew:

> *"Go therefore and make disciples of all the nations, baptizing the in the name of the Father and of the Son and of the Holy Spirit."* **Matthew 28:19 (KJAV)**

The first apologetic of Christian Trinitarianism was that of Quintus Septimius Florens Tertullian[lxiii] (155-240

C. E.) of Carthage in the Roman Province of North Africa. Trinitarianism is not unique to Christianity. There had been pre-Christian Trinitarianism in India, Mesopotamia, Egypt, and Greece. Its pagan antecedence should not be a reason to oppose it, because most religions have antecedents in other religions. Jewish monotheism, for example, has its antecedent in the monotheism of Pharaoh Akhenaten, known also as Amenhotep IV.

Arthur Weigalls, a religious writer that trashes all Christian doctrines which have pagan derivatives, quotes Aristotle to link Christian Trinitarianism to paganism:[lxiv]

> *"All things are three, and thrice is all: and let us use this number in the worship of the gods; for, as the Pythagorians say, everything and all things are bounded by threes, for the end, the middle and the beginning have this number in everything, and these compose the number of the Trinity."*

Although it is tempting to associate Christian Trinitarianism with Aristotelean logic, it is important to know that Weigalls disparages all religions that are derived from a previous other. Few, if any, religions are altogether original. The three Abrahamic religions, namely Judaism, Christianity, and Islam, used Aristotelian logic in the tenth through thirteenth centuries to boost the dialectic methodology of their theology.

That a teenage Jewish virgin or young woman is the mother of God (YHWH) is a stumbling block to the rapport of Christians and Jews. Christians believed that the "Sovereign One" that spoke to Moses from a burning bush and thunderously gave him the Decalogue, became a human baby. The first Christians were converts from Judaism. That ought to have established rapport with the Jewish community. The apostle Paul, also a convert from Judaism, was such a radical departure from Judaism that it seemed like a burning of the bridge. He told the Philippians in a letter, that God emptied Himself into Mary's womb, where it gestated as the baby Jesus (Phil. 2:6-8).

Fifty days after the crucifixion of Jesus of Nazareth, His devotees bravely witnessed with their lives (martyrdom) to proclaim that the crucified and risen Jesus is Lord. Soon thereafter, large demographies at Jerusalem, Antioch in Syria, and as far east and west as India and Rome, respectively--and probably in Spain believed that Jesus of Nazareth was Lord and God. They gathered for a Thanksgiving fiesta every first day of the week. Eastern Christianity refers to the post-resurrection era as a perpetual "eighth day".[lxv] Many disciples testified that He appeared to them multiple times after the resurrection. On the occasion of the appearances, He reinforced the commission to go and preach and teach all people everywhere. When they gathered for Eucharist – the thanksgiving sacramental fiesta, they read the Scriptures, broke bread, and sipped red wine to remember Jesus' last feast with the Twelve.

The courage of the Christians spooked Emperor Trajan (98-117 C.E). It drove him to paranoia. Martyrdom or the ultimate witness to belief in the divinity of Jesus had become a crown of glory to many Christians. Many felt it was an obligation to replicate what Jesus Christ did for them. Emperor Trajan banned private clubs and social groups to stifle the enthusiasm of Christian. His action prevented the development of a Fire Brigade in Rome. Although the persecution of Christians was sporadic, it made their lives a living hell. It however spurred enthusiasm. The parents of Origen of Alexandria hid his clothes to restrain his juvenile propensity for martyrdom.

Tacitus said that Emperor Nero may have prosecuted Christians to divert attention from the whispering rumors that he (Nero) torched the City of Rome for urban renewal. Mariam Griffin suggests that arson was not probable given that there was a full moon only two days earlier. She suggested that although Jesus and Christians were equally detestable to the Roman authority, the Christians were scapegoat because Empress Poppaea was a Jewish sympathizer.[lxvi]

Flavius Josephus, who was born in 37 C.E., mentioned twelve men named Jesus in his Antiquities, two of whom fit the description of Jesus of Nazareth. He commented:

> *"About this time there lived Jesus, a wise man, if indeed one ought to call a man wise. For he was one who performed surprising deeds and was a teacher of such people as accept the truth gladly. He won over many Jews and many of the Greeks. He was the Messiah. And when, upon the accusation of the principal men among us, Pilate had condemned him to the cross, those who had come to love him did not cease. He appeared to them [after] spending a third day restored to life, for the prophets of God had*

*foretold these things and a thousand other marvels
about him. And the tribe of the Christians,
so called after him, has still to this day not
disappear.*[lxvii]

Josephus commanded a Jewish faction inside Jerusalem in the 65-70 C.E. insurrection against Rome and became an advisor to Emperors Vespasian and Titus after he was subsequently pardoned by Vespasian. Some wonder whether a Jew could give an unbiased opinion of Jesus. Some others said he wrote glowingly of Christians and copies of the Antiquities relating to Christianity were preserved by Christians.[lxviii]

Tacitus wrote that a man who prophesied against the Temple was brought to Pilate and that:

*"Christus, from whom the name (Christians)
had its origin, who suffered the extreme penalty
during the reign of Tiberius at the hand of one
of our procurators, Pontius Pilate, and a most
mischievous superstition . . . broke out not only in
Judah.... but even in Rome where all things hideous
and shameful from every part of the world find their
center and become popular."*[lxix]

Pilate decided that Jesus was harmless, although somewhat deranged and annoying to the Temple priests. He went on to say that Pilate had him flogged and released.

Two canonical Gospels--the Gospel according to Mark (16:19) and the Gospel according to Luke (24:51) said that He ascended from earth to heaven in the sight of eleven disciples. They were told to tarry in Jerusalem until they received power. The Gospel according to John (20:24-29) reported that the disciple Thomas doubted that Jesus had risen from death. That element of doubt may have been inserted to suggest that the story of the Easter moment was not a journalistic fait accompli. That one or more disciple doubted that Jesus rose from death give the narrative more credibility. Thomas has been credited as the probable evangelist that planted what became the Mar Toma Orthodox Church in South India. He may have hesitated to get the story right before he jumped on board and became a confessor.

Citing the Gospels according to Matthew and Luke that the fullness of God was implanted in the womb of Mary and developed a human body, and the Gospel according to John (1:1-14) that the Word (God) became flesh and lived as a human being, Christianity developed the Doctrine of the Divine Incarnation--a doctrine that God became Jesus of Nazareth and sacrifice himself to save humanity. Christianity has many creedal forms, the oldest being, "Jesus is Lord." The apostle Paul told his Corinthian converts to Christianity:

> *"If you confess that Jesus is Lord and believe that*
> *God raised him from the dead, you will be saved."*
> **(Rom. 10:9, GNB-TEV)**

Paul also cited that confession in the Epistle to the Philippians (Phil. 2:11). Baptism in the name of the

Lord Jesus is a confession that Jesus Christ is God (Acts 8:16 and I Cor. 6.11). From the simple creedal statement "Jesus is Lord", the church developed a comprehensive credal statement in the Apostles' Creed probably by the first decade of the second century. It apparently answers the question, "What happens to those who lived and died without hearing the Christian Gospel?"[lxx]

> *"I believe in God almighty (the Father almighty), and in Jesus Christ, his only Son, our Lord. Who was born of the Holy Spirit and the Virgin Mary; who was crucified under Pontius Pilate and was buried (descended to Hell). And the third day rose from the dead; who ascended into heaven, and sitteth on the right hand of the Father. Whence he cometh to judge the living and the dead; and in the Holy Ghost; the remission of sins; the resurrection of the flesh; the life everlasting."*

A Liberal Theological Movement of the 1960s coined the phrase, "Religionless Christianity,"[lxxi] which is an oxymoron, because Christianity is a religion. It is a worshipping community. The cross or crucifix and Christus Rex are important symbols of Christianity and Christian worship. The quest of the historical Jesus stimulates evangelism, because it pulls Christianity from the cultic closet to expose the historical Jesus of Nazareth for scrutiny.

German theologian Jurgen Moltmann believes that Trinitarianism predated the birth of Jesus of Nazareth and the events of the Triduum (Good Friday to Easter Day). He went on to say that there *was a cross in the heart of God before the cross was raised up on Golgotha*,[lxxii] but that that cross was revealed only in the life and death of Jesus Christ. Moltmann made Jesus of Nazareth the epicenter of community. He emphasized that community is "the opposite of both poverty and property." Community is not associated with the concepts of having and not having. Christian community specifically is associated with God, and God is Emanuel--with human beings as Jesus of Nazareth. God is One (monotheism) and God is also a community (Trinity). God revealed loving kindness in self-abasement to save humanity from pain, anxiety, death, and the "Ancient Prince of Hell" by becoming human.

Moltman went on to say that Christian *monotheism is expressed as Trinitarianism, and that Trinitarianism is the expression of a compassionate monotheism.* God as Trinity suggests that God is all things to all people. The prophet Isaiah saw the greatness of God in a vision the year that King Uzziah died. God was high and lifted up. Christian Reformer Martin Luther saw God--the same God that Isaiah saw coming among ordinary people and said, "*When you humble me, you make me great.*"[lxxiii] The prophet Isaiah and Luther saw God as King as well as peasant, and Abraham Hershel's religious experience of the awesomeness of God as King and Redeemer evoked the response of wonder:

> "*Your self-abasement shows me that you are great.*"[lxxiv]

Christianity combines majesty and abasement. There is the high and lifted-up Father and the debased humanity of God, Jesus Christ. Paul of Tarsus began the process of systematizing Christianity. The divine kenosis or self-emptying of God (Phil. 2:7) showcases humility as the supreme virtue. God as Jesus of Nazareth embodies both finite humanity and divine infinity.

The Greek word (παρθενοσ), is translated to English as "*Young woman*" as well as "Virgin", but the Christian Church chooses to translate it as "virgin" because virgin connotes greater purity than maiden or young woman. The prophet Isaiah in his messianic prophecy used the Hebrew word, "almah," which is invariably translated as "virgin" in the English Bible.

> *"Behold a virgin shall conceive, and bear a son, and shall call his name Immanuel."* **Isaiah 7:14 (KJAV)**

The Gospels according to Matthew and Luke suggest that the Nativity of Jesus of Nazareth is a fulfillment of that prophecy. The Matthean version of the annunciation reads:

> *"An angel of the Lord appeared to him (Joseph) in a dream and said, 'Joseph son of David, do not be afraid to take Mary home as your wife, because what is conceived in her is from the Holy Spirit."*
> - **Matthew 1:20 (NIV)**

The Lukan version reads,

"The angel went to her and said, 'Greetings, you are highly favored! The Lord is with you . . . you will be with child and give birth to a son, and you are to give him the name Jesus. . . . The Lord God will give him the throne of his father David, and he will reign over David's descendants forever."
- Luke 2:28, 31-33 (NIV)

Paul referred to the mother of Jesus Christ only as a woman (γυναιχηοσ), saying:
"But when the right time finally came, God sent his own Son. He came as the son of a human mother and lived under the Jewish Law."
Galatians 4:4 (GNB-TEV)

References to brothers and sisters of Jesus in the Gospels according to Matthew (13:55-57) and Mark (6:3) are distractions from the adoration of the perpetual virgin. They probably refer to children of Joseph from a previous marriage. St. Jerome suggested that the word (Greek: 'αδελπηοι' or Latin: 'fratres' could be translated as "cousins", but that is never a biblical usage. The Greek word for cousin is "νεπσιοσ" (nepsios). He would have been right if he said that Jesus understood kinship differently. When the disciples told him that His mother and brothers were waiting to talk with Him (Matt. 12:47-49), He said:

"For whoever shall do the will of My Father which is in heaven, the same is my brother and sister, and

mother." **Matt. 12:50 (KJAV)**

The reference to brothers and sisters is not necessary and could have been omitted. They climbed on to the Jesus of Nazareth bandwagon only when the Jesus movement became a fan club.

That Mary was "a perpetual virgin" has been a subject of discourse and debate by Christians and non-Christians alike. Joseph was the surrogate father and babysitter of Jesus. He was obviously a virtuous celibate spouse. The association of virginity and purity as religious virtues were the probable reasons for the establishment of monasteries and convents.

The Incarnation of God (YHWH-Elohim) in the prologue to the Gospel according to John, happened without a human parent. God simply became human. The Word became flesh. The essence of divinity became human and that which was transcendent became imminent:

> *"In the beginning the Word already existed; the Word was with God; and the Word was God. From the beginning the Word was with God. Through him God made all things."* **John 1:1-3 (GNB-TEV)**

Although Jesus of Nazareth is not mentioned in that prologue, He is implied. People who believe that Jesus is divine become, like Him, "Children of God." They are an apparent chosen people begotten by God without human parents.

> *"Some, however, did receive him and believed in him; so He gave them the right to become God's children. They did not become God's children by natural means, that is, by being born as the children of a human father; God himself was their Father."*
> – John 1:12-13 (GNB-TEV)

This text implies that God raises those who believe that Jesus is Lord to the status of divinity. All Christians have become divine (holy) through Jesus Christ. The Church is like the womb of Mary and Christians pass through it in the process of becoming saints. Christians comprise the body of Jesus Christ and as such are co-redeemers with Jesus Christ. They are already saints. Jesus Christ as God is always faithful to those who receive Him as their Lord and God.

Writing to the Christians in Galatia, the Apostle Paul juxtaposed two texts; Deuteronomy 21:13 & Galatians 3:13, to show the saving power of God. Whereas the Old Covenant said that "a hanged man is accursed by God" (Deut. 21:13), the New Testament citing the crucifixion of Jesus of Nazareth on a tree (cross) said that the hanging of Jesus on a cross (tree) erased the curse imposed by the Law (Gal. 3:13-14). That is another instance that Christianity understood itself to be a development of Judaism. God restores humanity to wholeness in Christianity.

An epistle supposedly written by the apostle Simon (Peter) tells us that Jesus Christ preached to souls that were trapped in Hades (Hell) while He was domiciled in the sepulcher--between Good Friday and Easter. The assumption is that He was an active Lord even in the tomb.

> *"That is why the Good News was preached also to the dead... they may live as God lives."*
> **I Peter 4:6 (GNB-TEV)**

The Anglican Communion adopts the Trinitarian phrase, "Three-legged stool" to frame its comprehensive understanding of salvation. The concept of the three things necessary for salvation is explained as:
1. Holy Scriptures
2. Tradition
3. Human Reason

The Judeo-Christian Scriptures of the Old and New Testament is central to the Christian doctrine of salvation. Tradition refers to the way the Church used and interpreted the Scriptures through the centuries. The church believes that God has endowed human beings with intelligence and expects them to use and apply that gift appropriately. The disciples that Jesus left behind when He left the earth, are guardians of His spiritual legacy. They proclaimed it and protected it from extraneous religious and philosophical pollution.

Emperors Constantine I and Licinius issued the Edict of Toleration in 313 C. E. made all religious cults tolerable within the bounds of the Roman Empire. Constantine elevated Christianity to the status of first among the religions of the Empire in 324 C.E., and Emperor

Theodosius I issued the Edict of Thessalonica in 380 C.E., which made Nicaean Christianity the State religion. That Edict gave special privileges to Christianity. Bishops were officials of the state. Those edicts energized Christianity and the Church grew phenomenally. There was, however, some negative consequences. The phenomenal growth and privileged position of the clergy made many of them haughty and oftentimes intransigent when issues of doctrinal differences arose. They were also compromised as officials of the state. Although the Emperor enforced the mandates of the church councils, the officialdom perpetuated conflict. Imperial intervention to manage ecclesiastical conflicts became the norm.

Little is known about life in the local congregations, especially in the regions where most of the Christians were barely literate or illiterate. Erudite ecclesiastical scholastics like the Cappadocian fathers, Ignatius of Antioch, John Chrysostom, and Athanasius of Alexandria, and Tertullian of Carthage among others, may have been meaningful only at the courts of secular and ecclesiastical princes. The sermons that survived were apparently preached in cathedrals to educated nobles, monks, and the middle-class rising to nobility.

Creeds became a necessity to manage doctrinal conflicts among them. The church councils were the battle grounds of bishops who were trained in philosophy, rhetoric, and philology. That may have been a reason for their intransigence. They claimed superior understanding of the person of Jesus Christ over their peers. Seven Ecumenical Councils have been recognized by Anglicans

(Episcopal Church USA), Eastern Orthodox, Lutherans, Roman Catholic, and the Old Catholic Church.

The Athanasian Creed is retained as a historical document in the Episcopal Church's (Anglican) Book of Common Prayer. It is an embodiment of everything in the Nicene Creed. The source is anonymous. Known in Latin as *Quicunque Vult* because of its opening words, "Whoever wishes," it avoids the errors of subordination and tritheism and attributes divinity to each of the persons of the Trinitarian godhead, namely: Father, Son (Jesus of Nazareth), and Holy Spirit. Each is uncreated (increatus), limitless (immensus), eternal (aeternus), and omnipotent (omnipotens). First mentioned in the Minutes of the Fourth Council of Toledo in 633 C.E., it defines salvation as redemption from sin, which is the essence of the Christian doctrine of salvation. This creed was named "Athanasian" because its Christology is like that of Athanasius of Alexandria.

A major focus of the disputations at the Ecumenical Councils of the Church has been "How does Jesus of Nazareth save mankind from Sin?" The divinity as well as the humanity of Jesus of Nazareth are equally imperative factors for Him to save sinners from sin.

I was once invited by the pastor of a rural Pentecostal congregation in Southeastern Jamaica, West Indies, to lead a Bible study--which turned out to be an intense spiritual experience. They sang intermittently, either to keep the congregation awake or to help them to digest each segment of the teaching I gave. The lyric of the song was:

*"I do believe I must believe that Jesus died for me.
Upon the cross He shed His blood from sin to set me free."*

It was their creedal statement. They believed that Jesus died for them--I could see it in their faces and felt in my heart that they were willing to die as witnesses to the Lordship of Jesus Christ.

13

ECUMENICAL COUNCILS

THE FIRST ECUMENICAL COUNCIL: NICAEA I (325 C. E.)

Daniel Defoe, Martin Luther, and Bishop Ken of Bath and Wells poetically pass along this poetic statement, the origin of which is apparently anonymous:

> *"Whenever God erects a house of prayer, the devil always builds a chapel there, and 'twill be found upon examination; the latter has the larger congregation."*

As previously stated, religious freedom in the fourth century C.E. was both a blessing and a cause for concern. Every man seemed to mount his own religious soap box. Arius, an Alexandrian cleric, taught what was known as the Antiochene heresy – that although Jesus of Nazareth may have pre-existed the incarnation, He was not co-eternal with the Father. He argued that Jesus of Nazareth may have been the Son of God, but being begotten of the Father in time, there was a time when He was not. That made Jesus necessarily subordinate to God the Father.

Arius and the Antiochenes overemphasize the humanity of Jesus. The Alexandrians, on the other hand, emphasized his divinity; "The Word became flesh." Arius taught that Jesus Christ is necessary, because God is great and incommunicable: hence the need for a mediator between God and human beings.[lxxv] That is the Christology of many evangelical preachers. There is a tendency to see Jesus as the medium through which one must go to get to God. Like Arius, they believe that Jesus was created and came into being in time even if He is the "only begotten Son of the Father."

Alexander, the archbishop of Alexandria rejected Arius' doctrine of the subordination of Jesus Christ to God the Father. Unable to rein in the enthusiasm of Arius and the doctrinal frenzy which became known as the Arian Controversy, he appealed for help to his fellow bishops. Because the controversy threatened the unity of the Christian Church and the Roman Empire, Emperor Constantine intervened. The bishops welcomed Constantine's judicial intervention in the conflict. He proactively summoned the bishops throughout the Roman Empire to an Ecumenical Council at Nicaea (Iznik), in present day Turkey. He guaranteed safe conduct to and from the Council. About three hundred bishops and their aids attended.

The Emperor convened the Council, and Bishop Hosius of Cordova, who was his religious advisor, presided. The Council supported Alexander's deposition of Arius but apparently had difficulty moving forward. Some erudite bishops, including Eusebius of Caesarea, initially supported Arius. Athanasius, then a deacon and theological advisor to Bishop Alexander, mentioned that bishops sarcastically winked at each other in amusement at the apparent confusion.

The introduction of the Greek word "ομοουσιοσ" (homoousios), a word that means "same substance" or that Jesus of Nazareth (Christ) was of the same substance as God the Father was the game changer. Tertullian of Carthage had used the phrase "unius substantiae"[lxxvi] and Hosius of Cordova probably saw "homoousius" as a convenient translation of Tertullian's phrase "unius substantiae." Hosius may have suggested the word to the Emperor, and the Emperor may have suggested that should the Council employ the word "Homoousia," it could solve the problem of Arianism. Alexander of Alexandria accepted "Homoousios" as sufficiently anti-Arian. Homoousios surfaced in debates at regional councils over the past sixty years[lxxvii] as a possible defining word for the Christology of the western church but had been consistently rejected. The Council examined the Baptismal creeds from the church at Jerusalem and Caesarea among others and prepared a creed into which they inserted the word "Homoousios." The Council substituted the word "Son" for "Logos," the clauses "Came down from heaven," and "was made Man," were added to safeguard the mystery of the incarnation. It omitted "First begotten of all creation"[lxxviii] though Scriptural, fearing that the Arians could reconstruct and use it to support the doctrine of subordination. The Council accepted it after much discussion.

Arius may not have set out to be a troublemaker. He probably was not primarily concerned with whether the Father and the Son is the same. His concern may have been the nature of salvation from sin. Irenaeus of Lyons two centuries earlier said, "*What was not assumed by the Savior is not redeemed . . . the glory of God is the human being fully alive.*" He probably read into Irenaeus' statement of faith that salvation through Jesus is contingent on Jesus becoming like those for whom He came to save. Given that concern, Arius and his supporters necessarily disagreed with the Nicaean Christology, because Nicaea formulated a Christology of unity of the Father and the Son in a way that ignored the link between Jesus and the rest of humanity.[lxxix]

The Creed coming from the Council affirmed the following seven-fold doctrinal formula:[lxxx]

i. *That Jesus was a human being who was also fully God.*
ii. *That Jesus came into the world as the son of only one earthly parent, Mary.*
iii. *That Jesus never sinned or did anything wrong.*
iv. *That agents of Judaism accused Jesus of heresy and handed him over to the Romans who crucified him.*
v. *He was buried in a tomb and rose from the dead on the third day.*
vi. *He ascended to God the Father.*
vii. *He will return to earth.*

Conferees were apparently pressured into accepting the doctrinal formula that "God the Father and Jesus of Nazareth is of the same substance." Eusebius of Caesarea who initially supported Arius, voted with the majority to affirm the Nicaean Christology.

Although Alexander had taken an outline of a creed to the Council, the exemplar at the Council was probably the Baptismal Creed of Eusebius of Caesarea. Hans Lietzmann opined that it was the Creed of Jerusalem. Whatever its origin, the following is the Creed which the Council adopted, and the Emperor endorsed:

"We believe in One God the Father All-sovereign, maker of all things visible and invisible; and in one Lord Jesus Christ, the Son of God, begotten of the Father, only begotten, that is, of the substance of the Father; God of God, Light of Light, true God of true God, begotten, not made, of one substance with the Father; through whom all things were made, things in heaven and things on the earth; who for us men and for our salvation came down, and was made flesh, and became man, suffered, and rose again on the third day, ascended into the heavens, is coming to judge living and dead. And in the Holy Spirit."[lxxxi]

The Council also handed down anathema (condemnations) on anyone who said,

"There once was when he was not," and "before he was begotten he was not," and that; "he came to be from things that were not . . . another hypostasis. (Greek): substantia (Latin) that the Son of God is subject to change or alteration."

THE SECOND ECUMENICAL COUNCIL: CONSTANTINOPLE I (381 C.E.)

The number of Arians surged during the reign of Constantius (350-361) and Julian (361-363 C.E.), respectively. Some Arians showed willingness to compromise and proposed the word "Homoiousius" in lieu of "Homoousius" at a regional Council in 359 C.E. The Orthodox Nicaean party rejected "Homoiousius," which means "similar." The Nicaean Orthodox party demanded compliance with the sameness (Homoousius) of substance of the Father and the Son.

The Christological controversy was further complicated when Apollinaris of Laodicea began teaching that Jesus Christ had a human body, but His mind was divine. According to Apollinaris, Jesus felt pain and experienced emotions because He had a human body, but His mind, which was divine, was the source of thinking, doing miracles, rising from the dead to life, and other spiritual activities. Apollinarianism like Arianism subordinated the human Jesus of Nazareth to God the Father.

Emperor Theodosius the First, who made Christianity the official religion of the Roman Empire in the year 380 C.E., convened the Second Ecumenical Council in 381

C.E. to resolve the lingering Arian and the Apollinarian heresies. A hundred and fifty bishops attended the first Council of Constantinople. Most of them were from the Eastern section of the Empire. The Roman Church did not participate officially, but it had some influence in the decision making. Among the changes it influenced are:

a. Added the "Filioque Clause,"[lxxxii] which meant that the Holy Spirit proceeds from the Father **and the Son.** Some wonder whether the "Filioque clause" is necessary. Jorgen Moltmann thinks it is because the Father shines through the Son, and makes the Father and the Son the one subject from which the Holy Spirit proceeds.[lxxxiii] The Eastern Orthodox Church retains the Holy Spirit proceeds from the Father **through the Son."**

b. **Added the** phrase "Deum de Deo" or "God from God." "Deum de Deo" (God from God) affirms the Nicaean formula that Jesus of Nazareth is divine.

c. **Amended or changed** the phrase, "We believe . . ." to read, "I believe . . ." It makes faith more personal.

Ambrose, Bishop of Milan (died 397 C.E.), taught that Jesus had a human nature and a divine nature--the human does what is natural to human while the divine does what is natural to divinity--and that the Son is wholly united to the Father and thus equal to the Father. Nicaea mandated that the two natures function as a union. Ambrose's Christology seems to suggest some level of independence of the human and the divine natures. His Christology was stated slightly different from that at Nicaea I, but it apparently passed the orthodoxy test.

THE THIRD ECUMENICAL COUNCIL: EPHESUS (431 C.E.)

On becoming the Metropolitan or archbishop of Constantinople in 328 C. E., Nestorius mediated a controversy between two clergy factions. One faction taught that God was born as a man in Jesus Christ, and that Mary is the Theotokos (Θεοτοκοσ) or the Mother of God. The other faction taught that God is eternal and could not have been born. That faction denied the divinity of Jesus of Nazareth. Nestorius attempted to chart a middle course. He said that Mary was properly the mother of the Messiah (Christ) and is Christotokos. His Christology fell short of affirming the Nicaean and Constantinopolitan Christology that Jesus Christ is "God from God." Assuming the authenticity of a Nestorian apologetic discovered in the early decades of the 20th century, Nestorius confided that "Christotokos" was acceptable to both sides of the controversy as an appropriate title for Mary the Mother of Jesus, until there was outside interference.[lxxxiv] That outside interference may have been the Western (Roman) Church and Cyril of Alexandria.

Much of the conflict in the Christian Church was rooted in the socio-political issues in the Roman Empire. The bishop of Rome had the ears of the Emperor and had an amicable relationship with the Metropolitan (bishop) of Alexandria. The Emperor of the West moved the Capital from Rome to Constantinople around 337 C.E., and the Metropolitan (bishop) of Constantinople claimed equality or second in status to the city of Rome. Alexandria and Constantinople competed for the status of Second City of the Empire.

When Emperor Arcadius named John (Chrysostom) of Antioch as the Metropolitan (archbishop) of Constantinople in 397 C.E., the decision irked Theophilus, the Metropolitan (archbishop) of Alexandria (385-412). The candidate proposed to the emperor by Theophilus was overlooked. Tensions heightened between Constantinople and Alexandria.

In rejecting the proposition that Mary is the mother of God, Nestorius and his supporters also denied that God could be a baby of one or two days old, or that Jesus Christ could be consubstantial or share substance with God the Father. He proposed that should God and Jesus be consubstantial, God could grow old, suffer, and die; things that are not proper for God.

Nestorius was first summoned on a deposition of Cyril of Alexandria to a Council in Rome in August 430 C.E. Cyril presided at that Council and Nestorius' Christology (Doctrine of the relationship of Jesus of Nazareth and God) was condemned and he was deposed. The Synod of Rome (430 C.E.) issued an ultimatum to Nestorius to recant within ten days or be exiled. Nestorius ignored the ultimatum and appealed the deposition to the Eastern Emperor Theodosius II. Valentinian III (Western) and Theodosius II (Eastern) summoned the bishops to an Ecumenical Council; the third ecumenical council. It met at Ephesus in 431 C.E. The Council of Ephesus removed Nestorius from his powerful and prestigious office as bishop of Constantinople and exiled him to Petra, located in the Arabian Desert, and then to the great Oasis in Egypt.[lxxxv] While in Egypt, Nestorius may have written *The Bazaar of Heracleides* under a pseudonym.[lxxxvi] The Council issued twelve anathema. The following three anathema express the Christology of the Council.

a. "If any one does not acknowledge that Emanuel is the True God, and that the holy Virgin is, in consequence, 'Theotokos,' for she brought forth after the flesh the Word of God who has become flesh, let him be anathema."

b. If any one does not acknowledge that the Word which is from God, the Father, was personally united with flesh, and with his own flesh is one Christ, that is, one and the same God and man together, let him be anathema.

c. If any one does not confess that the Word of God suffered in the flesh and was crucified in the flesh . . . let him be anathema.[lxxxvii]

The Council's usage of the phrase "Mother of God," meant something different to that of Meister Eckhart which expressed his mystical experiences; "*We are all meant to be mothers of God, for God always needs to be born in us."* The Ecumenical Council of Ephesus meant it literally.

THE FOURTH ECUMENICAL COUNCIL: CHALCEDON (451 C.E.)

The Fourth Ecumenical Council was the response to what is known as the Monophysite Heresy. The protagonist was Eutyches, an archimandrite or head of a large monastery outside of the city of Constantinople. He taught that Jesus had only one nature--the divine nature. Although Bishop Leo of Rome suggested to the Emperor that the Council venue be in the Western Empire, Byzantine Emperor Marcian said the issue of Monophysitism was primarily an issue of the Eastern Church. The Council convened on October 8, 451 C.E., with a suggestion that Bishop Paschasinus of Sicily preside. The suggestion that the bishop of Sicily preside at the Council of Chalcedon was made to thwart any ambitious effort of Dioscorus of Alexandria to seize control of the Council. The purpose of the Council was to respond to the Monophysite heresy.

The Council heard a reading of the decrees of the Ecumenical Councils of Nicaea and Constantinople I; the formula of Union agreed to by John of Antioch, Cyril of Alexandria, and the Tome of Leo. A representative of the Emperor announced to the Council on October 22 that the Emperor wanted a statement of faith or he would move the Council to the west side of the Empire. The Council appointed a Committee of twelve, which included three from Rome. The Council mandated:

a. Reaffirmation of the Nicene Creed. It included anti-Arian statements made necessary by issues at the Councils of Nicaea and Constantinople I.
b. Confirmation of the deposition of Nestorius.
c. It condemned Eutychian Monophysitism.
d. The Council mandated that Constantinople had the same status as Rome. The Emperor attempted to veto it but approved it with the amendment that Rome had primacy.[lxxxviii]

The doctrinal statement coming from the Council of Chalcedon is known as Dyophytism. The pro-Cyril delegates pushed for greater emphasis on "hypostatic union." It was a compromise that merged the Alexandrian and the Antiochene Christology. Neither the Eastern nor the Western Church was satisfied with the compromise. The Antiochenes accepted the Christological formula that Mary is theotokos or Mother of God. The Council also accepted that Mary was the Temple from which Jesus received his manhood. The Creedal statement from Chalcedon reads:

> *"Wherefore, following the holy Fathers, we all with one voice confess our Lord Jesus Christ one and the same Son, the same perfect in Godhead, the same perfect in manhood, truly God and truly man, the*

same consisting of a reasonable soul and a body, of one substance with the Father as touching the Godhead, the same of one substance with us as touching the manhood, like us in all things apart from sin; begotten of the Father before the ages as touching the Godhead, the same in the last days, for us and for our salvation, born from the Virgin Mary, the Theotokos, as touching the manhood, one and the same Christ, Son, Lord, Only-begotten, to be acknowledged in two natures, without confusion, without change, without division, without separation; the distinction of natures being in no way abolished because of the union, but rather the characteristic property of each nature being preserved . . . even as the Prophets from the beginning spoke concerning him, and our Lord Jesus Christ instructed us, and the Creed of the Father has handed down to us.[lxxxix]

THE FIFTH ECUMENICAL COUNCIL: CONSTATINOPLE II (553 C. E.)

The Arian controversy intensified in the third decade of the sixth century. The Empress Theodora supported Monophysitism and engineered the election of Vigilius[xc] as Bishop of Rome in 537. He remained the bishop of Rome until 555 C.E. Monophysites vigorously opposed Arianism and Nestorianism. There were whispers that many who were declared orthodox by the Council of Chalcedon were Nestorians and Arians. Monophysites began to examine the Christology of

Origen and his second-century Alexandrian companions. Origen cited Luke (17: 21) and suggested that the divine Spirit implanted in humans may purify and give them perfect vision of God – a process that may result in union with God. He also suggested that the body of Jesus after the resurrection may have been only the form of a human body, but it was wholly **spiritual**, and that the form of the human body clothes the resurrected spirit. That doctrine suggests that the resurrected body is not a real human body.

The Alexandrians taught that although Jesus as Son of God was immutable or changeless and probably pre-existent, He was begotten by the will of God the Father--thus making Him less than equal with the Father. He may not have had human desires because He was sustained by divine power. Origen suggested that Jesus took on the human (sarx) nature at the incarnation and that the flesh may not have survived the death and resurrection. Nicaean Orthodoxy rejected the notion that the body is like clothes for the divine spirit or mind[xci] and that the Logos controlled the human body.

Emperor Justinian I summoned the bishops to the Second Council of Constantinople to resolve doctrinal controversies. Constantinople II reinforced what previous Councils had mandated; that Jesus of Nazareth is fully divine and fully human, and that neither the human nor the divine nature conflicted with the other or control the other. The Council also mandated that the ***body of Jesus is the same as any other human body and that it remained a real human body after the resurrection***. *It condemned those* *that taught that the resurrected body of Jesus was wholly spiritual or* that it was perfect, or unreal, or angelic, or non-human. In doing so it retroactively condemned the Christology of the Alexandrian philosophical theologians Origen, Theodore, and Clement.[xcii]

Origen's doctrine of the person of Jesus Christ was based on logic. The Orthodox Christology was mystic and ontological. The Council's mandate was oriented to faith; faith that the Incarnation did not add a new person to the Godhead because the Son existed eternally. The Council's theologians said that Origen's use of the word "begotten" implied that the incarnation added a nature.

Although Origen was not always consistent, his ethics and learning were admirable. He seemed so concerned about Christian ethics, that he emasculated himself after reading Jesus' admonition to his disciples about marital ethics (Matthew 19:12), and especially verse 12:

> *"For there are eunuchs who were born that way from their mother's womb, and there are eunuchs who are made eunuchs by men, and there are also eunuchs who made themselves eunuchs for the sake of the kingdom of Heaven."* **Matthew 19:12 (KJAV)**

What he taught was wholly accepted and praised during his lifetime, and the heresy did not become apparent for more than four hundred years after his death. Some suggest that he may have influenced Arius' and Nestorius' Christology, and that the heresy may have gone undetected but for the arrogance of Arius.

Anathema 5 of the eleven anathemas coming out of Constantinople II reads:

> *"If anyone understands the expression – one hypostasis of our Lord Jesus Christ – so that it means the union of many hypostases, and if he attempts thus to introduce into the mystery of Christ two hypostases, or two persons, and, after having introduced two persons, speaks of one person according to dignity, honor or worship, as Theodore and Nestorius insanely have written; and if anyone slanders the holy synod of Chalcedon, as though it had used this expression in this impious sense, and does not confess that the Word of God is united with the flesh hypostatically, and that therefore there is but one hypostasis or one person, and that the holy synod of Chalcedon has professed in this sense the one hypostasis of our Lord Jesus Christ; Let him be anathema. For the Holy Trinity, when God the Word was incarnate, was not increased by the addition of a person or hypostasis."* [xciii]

Emperor Justinian added his own anathema:

> *"If any says or thinks that the body of our Lord Jesus Christ was first formed in the womb of the holy virgin and that afterwards there was united with God the Word and the preexistent soul, let him be anathema."*

Augustine of Hippo was a Nicaean. He wrote:

"This is the sum of it all, that in the resurrection every man shall arise with the same body that he had, or would have had in his fullest growth, in all comeliness, and without deformity of any even the least member . . . shall arise in the proper stature of his growth which he had when he died."[xciv]

The Council was concerned that Origen's Christology portrayed Jesus of Nazareth as a Greek god. Rome supported the mandate of Constantinople II, but several western ecclesiastical jurisdictions rejected it: Northern Italy, England, France, Spain, Mediterranean-Africa, and Asia. That many western bishops did not vote with the Bishop of Rome, signaled the deflation of the power and influence of Rome with the western bishops. The influence of Rome vacillated. Opposition to the decision of Constantinople II ended in the Western Mediterranean in 559 C.E. Milan remained in Schism until 571 C.E. It is possible that imperial pressure was responsible for much of the compliance, but several of the dissenting bishops did not acquiesce to the mandate of Constantinople II until at the Sixth Ecumenical Council in 680 – 681 C.E.

THE SIXTH ECUMENICAL COUNCIL: CONSTANTINOPLE III (680-681)

Constantine IV (Byzantium) convened the sixth Ecumenical Council in Constantinople in response to the controversial teaching of Sergius (d. 638 C.E.). Sergius, the

Bishop of Constantinople from 610 to 638 C.E., unveiled the doctrine of Monothelitism in 622 C.E. He taught that Jesus had only one will-the divine will-- although He had two natures.

Heraclitus, the Emperor of the East (610-641 C.E.), was reticent to mediate the conflict probably because of the influence of his amicable relationship with Sergius who he had appointed a regent,[xcv] and his desire to appease the powerful Monophysite lobby. Sergius had rallied the people at Constantinople to support the Emperor and had presided at a solemn liturgy on Easter Day 622 to support the Emperor's march to war the following day. He ignored the potential for conflict associated with the doctrine of Monothelitism despite strong opposition to it from Sophronius, the patriarch of Jerusalem (629 C.E.) and a cadre of influential bishops of high population areas. Heraclitus was also weakened by the crumbling imperial organization. He had even contemplated moving his capital to Carthage, in North Africa.

He tried to broker a compromise between those who supported the mandate of the Council of Chalcedon and the Monothelites by substituting the word **Monoenergism** for **Monothelitism.** The philologically savvy bishops pushed back. Monothelitism means "one will" and Monoenergism means "one energy." Constantine IV (Byzantium 668-685 C.E.) decided that an Ecumenical Council was necessary to resolve the longstanding doctrinal controversy. The Council condemned Monoenergism and Monothelitism as heresies and mandated Dyophysitism.

Dyophysitism is the doctrine that Jesus Christ had a Divine will and a human will, and that both wills are autonomous and function in perfect harmony. The Antiochenes and pro-Origen theologians chose to teach that the preexistent souls fell from their primal states into matter and became angels, demons, and human beings. They taught that human bodies die, but it is inappropriate to say that the spirit or mind can die.

Eutychius of Constantinople who had been in exile 565-577 surfaced to deny the resurrection of the body. Gregory, the future bishop Gregory the Great of Rome, who had been an imperial legate in residence at the imperial court, got Emperor Tiberius to condemn what Eutychius taught. Tiberius forced Eutychius to burn the books containing the heresy. A teaching of Origen that there will not be any matter at the end of time was also anathema. The orthodoxy of Dyophysitism which had been mandated at Nicaea through Constantinople II was reaffirmed.

THE SEVENTH ECUMENICAL COUNCIL: NICAEA II (786-787 C.E.) (ICONOCLAST CONTROVERSY)

The Byzantine imperial court and the Eastern Church experienced two waves of iconoclasm, 726 C.E. until 787 C.E, and 814 C.E. until 842 C.E. Known as the Iconoclastic or icon breaking Controversy, (Greek: eikonoklasths), it began when vandals in the north began smashing icons. Soon the veneration of icons became a criminal offense in Byzantium.

The Veneration of Icons (images) was an affront to Muslims, and when Leo III (717-740 C. E.) began his reign facing a ferocious Muslim siege of Constantinople, the Byzantine imperial Court seriously considered the elimination of icons at court and in the church. Empress Irene and her son Constantine VI convened Nicaea II in 786 C.E. to quell the Controversy. The name "Eikonomachia" (Εικονομαχια) literally means "image struggle" or "war on icons". Christian, and Muslim iconoclasts cite Exodus 20:4 in support of their position.

Nicaea which hosted the First Ecumenical Council in 325 C.E., welcomed a large contingent of conferees again in 786 C.E. This Ecumenical Council was contemporaneous with the rise of Islamic militarism in the Middle East and Eastern Europe. Byzantium had been battered from the West and the East by Christian crusaders and the armies of Islam respectively. Most of the Byzantium bishops were iconoclasts and Empress Irene knew she had their support. John Damascene, however, disassociated from them citing his belief that icons have pedagogic value as visual aids and promotion of reverence and piety. The west was pro-icon. Gregory the Great (died 604 C.E.) of Rome rebuked Serenus, Bishop of Marseilles, for destroying icons saying:

"They are means of leading the illiterate to a knowledge of the truth of faith."

He also wrote to hermits who requested sacred images from him saying:

"I know that you do not seek the image of our Savior that you may worship it as God, by

*bringing to mind the Son of God you may keep
warm in the love of Him whose image you desire to
have before you. We bow before it not as divinity,
but we worship Him of whom we are reminded by
the picture that shows His birth or his throne.*[xcvi]

At an earlier date, Emperor Heraclitus carried an icon of Jesus ahead of his invading troops in Persia. He probably attributed power to the icon. Sergius painted icons on churches to protect them from invading Muslims. Byzantium Emperors were iconoclast and Gregory the Great of Rome dared him to remove the icon of Peter in Rome or to arrest him. Gregory's message to the emperor was:

*"You know that the dogmas of holy church are
not the concerns of emperors but of pontiffs who
ought to teach securely. The pontiff who presides
over the church do not meddle in affairs of state,
and likewise the emperors ought not to meddle in
ecclesiastical affairs."*[xcvii]

Gregory the Great who died in 731 felt strong enough to challenge the emperors. The Bishop of Rome was becoming more independent of the Emperor. Gregory's successor, Gregory II, convened the Synod of Rome which excommunicated the iconoclasts. That angered the emperor. He retaliated by levying higher taxes on properties in Italy. He also seized and transferred Roman church property in Italy to the Patriarch of Constantinople. Tension escalated in the Empire, and a schism between the Eastern and the Western Church seemed inevitable.

The argument of the Iconoclasts that an icon of Jesus Christ could only represent His humanity was Arianism, Origenism, and Nestorianism. The Council of Hieria in 754 excommunicated the Iconophiles. Violence erupted and a deposed patriarch was beheaded.

The business of Nicaea II began September 24, 787. The decrees of the Council were concise. An extract read:

> *"So, having made investigation with all accuracy and having taken counsel . . . 'With all certitude and accuracy that just as the figure of the precious and life -giving cross, so also the venerable and holy images, as well as painting and mosaic or other suitable materials, are to be exposed in the holy churches of God. . . the figure of our Lord God and Savior Jesus Christ, of our spotless Lady, the Mother of God. . .. For the honor which is paid to the image passes on to that which the image represents, and he who reveres the image reveres in it the subject represented."* [xcviii]

The bishops of Rome and of Constantinople signed the decree of the Council. It specified that icons were venerated but not worshipped. They are representations of real models that are physical like Jesus and Mary and the crucifixion. The Council also observed that the Scriptures of Judaism (Old Testament) approved an icon, the Ark of the Covenant, which was built of cypress wood and adorned with Seraphim and Cherubim and covered with a veneer of gold. The prayer of consecration of an icon in the Orthodox Church acknowledges the divine commandment not to worship any graven images. Athanasius of Alexandria refers to the ark as a symbol of the Virgin Mary:

> *"O noble Virgin, truly you are greater than them all! O (Ark of the) Covenant clothed with purity instead of gold!"* xcix

The seventh Ecumenical Council issued this, among other anathema:

> *"If anyone does not confess that Christ our God can be represented in His humanity, let him be anathema (condemned). If anyone does not accept representation in art or evangelical scenes let him be anathema. If anyone does not salute such representations as standing for the Lord and his saints let him be anathema. If anyone rejects any written or unwritten tradition of the Church let him be anathema."*

GOD EMPTIED "SELF" INTO A MAN

14

SUMMARY OF THE SEVEN ECUMENICAL COUNCILS AND THEIR MANDATES

The First through Seventh Ecumenical Councils of the Christian Church closely examined the Canonical Scriptures and answered the question, "Who is Jesus of Nazareth (Jesus Christ)?" Many bishops of the apostolic and post-apostolic church were schooled in philosophy and rhetoric, and they employed those skills and disciplines in their theological reflections and decision making. Bishops of rural and obscure diocese may not have understood the intricacies of the mandates and anathema of Councils. The Emperor and the Council were probably not concerned with that disconnect. The conciliar objective was to reduce conflict in the Church and the Empire. The church's objective ought to have been the enabling of evangelism. The Metropolitans (archbishops) probably paraphrased the decisions of the Councils to guide everyone to fulfill his/her obligation as Christian pastors.

NICAEA I: (325 C. E.) FIRST ECUMENICAL COUNCIL

MANDATE: (I) Jesus of Nazareth (Christ) is of the same Substance (Homoousia) as God the Father. **Full divinity** and full humanity affirmed.

(2) The incarnate Word eternally preexisted the Incarnation.

CONDEMNED: Arianism, which over-emphasized the humanity of Jesus of Nazareth.

CONSTANTINOPLE I: (380-381) SECOND ECUMENICAL COUNCIL AT CONSTANTINOPLE

MANDATE: Reaffirmed Nicaean formula that Jesus is **fully human** and fully Divine.

CONDEMNED Apollinarianism: The doctrine that Jesus had a human body, which is the seat of emotions and senses and a Divine Mind by which he did miracles and is raised from death.

EPHESUS I: (431 C. E.) THIRD ECUMENICAL COUNCIL WHICH MET AT EPHESUS

MANDATE: Reaffirms Nicaea and Constantinople 1 that Mary is the Mother of God.

CONDEMNED: Nestorianism, which denied the incarnation of God.

CHALCEDON: (451 C. E.) THE FOURTH ECUMENICAL COUNCIL

MANDATE: Dyophysitism. That Jesus Christ is One Person with two distinct natures joined in One Person, Jesus of Nazareth.

CONDEMNED: The Monophysite Heresy (an over-correction of the Nestorian Heresy), that Jesus' manhood was absorbed into His divinity.

CONSTANTINOPLE II: (551 C. E.) THE FIFTH ECUMENICAL COUNCIL

MANDATE: Reaffirmed the Unity of Person and the two natures of Jesus of Nazareth.

CONDEMNED:

    a. The Christology of Origen and Clement of Alexandria which suggests that God transformed the physical body of Jesus into a spiritual body after the resurrection from the dead; and uncertainty concerning the unity of the Father and the Son.

    b. Origen's doctrine of "Apokatastasis" or progressive purification of souls, a seeming series of reincarnation until the pure soul returns to the pure knowledge of God. It is de facto Neo-Platonism.

CONSTANTINOPLE III (SIXTH ECUMENICAL COUNCIL)

MANDATE: Jesus has two natures and two wills. The two wills function in perfect harmony.

CONDEMNED:

    a. Monothelitism; the doctrine that Jesus had two natures but only one will.

    b. Monoenergism. The heretical doctrine that Jesus Christ had two natures (divine and human), but only one energy.

NICAEA II: (SEVENTH ECUMENICA COUNCIL)

MANDATE: Icons are devotional and liturgical aids. Despite the Commandment against images (Exodus 20:4), Icons of Jesus of Nazareth, Mary His mother, and the saints are Appropriate because they are representations of actual human beings. That makes them pedagogically and liturgically efficacious. Paraphrased, they are good teaching visual aids and help worshippers to understand and make worship more efficacious. Icons of Jesus symbolize His humanity and divinity.

15

THE CONSISTENCY OF CHRISTOLOGY

Human thoughts and beliefs change over time, but the first seven Ecumenical Councils issued mandates and anathema that were consistent. There were umpteen regional councils that vacillated on issues, but the Ecumenical Councils were the battleground where the nature of God was determined and the foundation of Christianity as we now know it was laid. Those princes of the church were at times like rapacious beasts, but their pooled intellect and faith prepared the foundation of a resilient Christian church.

The First Ecumenical Council of Nicaea adopted a recommendation of Metropolitan Alexander of Alexandria that the Scriptures of Christianity are the foundation of all discourse about Christianity. The varied social context in which bishops did their ministry, and the many languages of the ecumenical dialog complicated the decision-making. Those were among the reasons for the many necessary follow-up regional and Ecumenical Councils. The goal was mutual acceptance of the Christological mandate.

The imperial court of Rome mandated that Christianity was the official religious faith of the Roman Empire in 324 C.E. Emperor made Christian clergy state officials in 380 C.E. The bishops remained in conflict about Jesus' person and natures. It is apparent that many of the conflicts arouse because of the miscommunication of delegates. They were probably saying the same thing and seem to disagree because of the different languages and cultures that mediated communication. Greek and Latin speaking delegates often misread the perspectives of the other. Although the bishops endeavored to support the mandates of previous councils, new ideas and arguments were introduced, which opened new controversies. The mandates have been that:

i. God became human (incarnation) as Jesus of Nazareth.
ii. Jesus of Nazareth is "One person with two natures; one human, the other divine.
iii. The Holy Trinity is One God in three persons, namely:
   (a) God the Father
   (b) God the Son (incarnate Jesus)
   (c) God the Holy Spirit
iv. Jesus of Nazareth (Jesus Christ) is one person of the undivided Trinity.
v. The three persons of the Godhead does not mean that there are gods

Pseudo-Dionysus has this interesting commentary on the Incarnation:

> *"Yet the goodness of the Deity has endless love for humanity and never ceased from benignly pouring out on us its providential gifts. It took up- on itself in a most authentic way all the characteristics of our nature, except sin. It became one with us in our lowliness, losing nothing of its own real condition, suffering no change or loss. It allowed us as those of equal birth, to enter into communion with it and to acquire a share of its own true beauty."* [c]

One may not know God without divine assistance. Jesus is both hidden as well as immanent in the Church. The incarnate God left the Church behind as the light in the world. The Church is the de facto reflector of the glory of God on to human beings. Those who believe that Jesus is the incarnation of God also believe that they are the bright shining image and likeness of God (2 Cor. 3:18, GNB- TEV).

GOD EMPTIED "SELF" INTO A MAN

16

WHO KILLED JESUS? PERSPECTIVE OF CHRISTIANITY

In an online quotation from *Christianity Today* dated August 1, 2000, Paul L. Maier said, "After centuries of censure, Jews have been relieved of the general responsibility of the death of Jesus." The Roman Church backtracked on anti-Semitism at the Second Vatican Council in 1965. The Council in the document Nostra Aetate said that the crucifixion of Jesus Christ could not be blamed on Jews as a whole. Roman Catholic Pontiff Benedict XVI in a March 2011 statement publicly affirmed the decision of Nostra Aetate.

Jerusalem Rabbi Eliezar Berkovits responded to the apparent shift in the understanding and relations of Roman Catholicism to Jews and Judaism with this comment: "In its effect upon the life of the Jewish people, Christianity's New Testament has been the most dangerous anti-Semitic tract in history." That may be true. Caution is advised on Christians and Jews going forward. Professor A. Roy Eckardt, of Lehigh University in Pennsylvania, who is also with the National Association of Christian and Jews, may be too enthusiastic in his desire for rapprochement of Christians and Jews. He suggested that Christianity edit out the crucifixion and resurrection of Jesus from the Christian Canon of Scriptures in order to erase the perception of anti-Semitism in Christianity. Eckardt's suggestion would mean the demise of Christianity. It would also be the catalyst for renewed anti-Semitism, especially from Evangelical Christians, who are currently the strongest segment of the Israeli lobby in the United States of America.

The death and resurrection of Jesus of Nazareth is indeed a major cause of anti-Semitism. The trial and crucifixion of Jesus of Nazareth in the Canonical Gospels, and especially in the Gospel according to John, and the writings of the Apostle Paul (Gal. 5:11) and (II Cor. 11:23-26), and the persecution of Christians by Jews reported in the Acts of the Apostles, has conditioned Christians to be prejudiced against Jews.

Fifth century Metropolitan Bishop John Chrysostom of Constantinople, a notable rhetorician, argued that the Jews only, and not the Romans, were guilty of murdering Jesus. Chrysostom may have been motivated by politics. Although he was critical of the empress among other people at the Imperial Court in his sermons, he was also a favored rhetorician of courtiers. His anti-Semitism and apparent apologetics for Rome may have been motivated by the desire to ingratiate himself to people at court. They were his patrons as well as members of his cathedral parish.

Arab Muslims who conquered Visigoth Christian Iberia in 711 C.E. initially forced the Iberian Christians to convert to Islam. Their grip on power faded between

1130 and 1481. The Spanish Inquisition (Roman Catholic) forced the Jews and Muslims to convert to Christianity beginning around 1391. Spanish Jews who resisted conversion to Christianity were expelled by Ferdinand and Isabella, the joint-monarchs of Spain (Aragon and Castile) in 1492. Many Jews in the Ukraine were also forced to convert to Eastern Orthodox Christianity.

ISLAM

Islam is the religion of Muslims. According to Reza Aslan, in "*No god but God: The Origins and Evolution of Islam,*" the Qur'an is the final revelation of God to man and Mohammad is the "Seal of the prophets." Aslan rebuts Max Weber's statement that, "Islam was never really a religion of salvation, Islam is a warrior religion," saying that the Qur'an does not annul the Scriptures of Judaism and Christianity but completes the revelation they began. She affirms that Islam is a religion of the Book and that the Scriptures of Judaism, Christianity, and Islam are related and from the same source. The prophet Mohammad and the Qur'an confirm that the Scriptures of the three faiths have a single exemplar, the Umm al-Kitab or "Mother of Books"[ci] (Quran 13:39), which is in heaven. Judaism, Christianity, and Islam are equally bellicose. See Jesus' discourse on swords (Matt. 26:51-52; Luke 22:34-38). The history of the Crusades and the wars of religions associated with the Reformation of Western Christianity in the 16th century bears that out. Aslan noted that Islam gestated in a hostile anti-Mohammad environment.[cii] It is also true that Arab Muslims initiated raids for profit against their neighbors.

Unfortunately, Islam is unfairly stereotyped especially in the Western world, as a warrior religion. The fact is that the Scriptures of Judaism, Christianity, and Islam all have sections with bellicose language. When Jesus told His disciples that they have heard it said, "An eye for an eye and a tooth for a tooth, but I say unto you, love your enemies" (Matt. 5:44), he was referring to the Torah (Ex. 21:24). The Qur'an alludes to "The eye for an eye" (Surah 2:5), which it said is the law laid down by God for the Jews. Islam's law of retaliation (Qisas) metes out punishment to the guilty in proportion to the magnitude of the victim's injury. A Saudi Arabian court sentenced an Egyptian man to force surgical removal of his left eye in 2000, after he was found guilty of damaging the eye of a 53-year-old man in an acid attack. (Specified in the Law of Hammurabi of Babylon about 2,000 B.C.E.) Another lost two teeth after he caused a like injury to a combatant in a fight.

Mohammad said that God sent the Torah to the Jews, Jesus was sent to affirm the Torah to Christians, and the Qur'an was given to the Arabs. That explains the single source and the alikeness of the three faiths. Mohammad revered Jesus[ciii] and acknowledged that Jews, Christians, and Muslims share a common origin. He also taught that their Scriptures laid the foundation that forms what he named "Monotheistic Pluralism."

The topic of Reza Aslan's book *There is no god but God* (There is no god but Allah), explains the meaning of the word "Allah." Let me reiterate what has been emphasized earlier in this book--Allah is an Arabic word which means god. It is sometimes used as a common noun and other times used as a proper noun referring to God. The name "Allah" has also been used by Christians and other religious groups as the name for God in Syria and adjacent countries in the Middle East. Some Judeo-Christians ask if Allah and YHWH can be used interchangeably. I hesitate to answer in the affirmative because linguistic differences have consequences when due care is not taken when people talk or write about faith and god.

If God gave the Torah to Moses, and Christians in the Orient knew God as Allah as well as YHWH, and Judaism, Christianity, and Islam accept the Torah as God's (YHWH) guide book, it is reasonable to conclude that the Torah is a sacred bridge to the three faiths. The major difference in the three Abrahamic faith communities is the extent to which they believe or understand that Jesus of Nazareth is related to God (YHWH/ALLAH).

Although Christianity and Islam teach that a virgin, Mary or Maryam, immaculately conceived and gave birth to a son and named him Jesus, the context in which the word "immaculate" is use is different. Immaculate means "without sin," and Western Christianity, following the lead of Augustine of Hippo, teaches that the sin of the first man (Adam) is transmitted venally through the father. Given the faith knowledge of Christianity and Islam that Mary (Maryam) conceived Jesus without a human father, Jesus was immaculately conceived (without sin).

The Qur'an tells us that Maryam was specially prepared to be the mother of Jesus. It does not say anything about Jesus' father. It implied, however, that she grew up in the Temple – having been dedicated to God by her parents.

In Islam, Jesus is only the Christ (Messiah) and prophet, but He is not divine. Islam denounces Christianity as polytheistic and suggests that Christians worship three gods. They refer to Jesus as another god. The following texts of the Qur'an apparently misrepresent core Christian teaching:

> "Some of you attribute partners to your Lord."[civ] **Surah 16:54**

and,

> "Do you not see how those given a share of the Scriptures, [evidently] now believe in idols and evil powers."
> **- Surah 4:51 (Abdel Haleem)**

Christianity (John 1) teaches that God became a human being; not that God (YHWH) unites with another God. It teaches that God the Son (Jesus) is eternal, but was only manifested as a human being when he became Mary's baby. The Qur'an said that the "People of the Book," which are Jews, Christians, and Muslims, ought to be modest in what they claim concerning Jesus of Nazareth, the Son of Mary (ibn-Maryam). Islam teaches that Jesus of Nazareth is only the messenger of God and the Messiah (al-Masih), but not God or the son of God. The Messiah or Christ or messiahs are human beings who have been anointed. Some messiahs are priests and kings, Jesus is therefore the Christ or Messiah of Christianity and Islam and an apostle or prophet of Allah (God) (Surah 4:171). Jesus and Mohammad are prophets of Islam. Mohammad is the ultimate Islamic prophet, which God (Allah) sent to restore faith after Jews and Christians corrupted it.[cv]

Muslims reject the notion that a person can save another person or that a person can pay the debt of others. Islam teaches that every person is responsible for his/her own misdeeds. Islam, therefore, does not credit Jesus of Nazareth to be the savior of the world.

Yasir Qadhi indicated that "when Muslim theologians mention sovereignty of their own tradition, they are not claiming that they are going to heaven and those following other paths are all damned. Rather, what they are asserting is that the path they follow leads to God's mercy, and they have no guarantee even about their own fate.[cvi] Muslims also reject the notion of vicarious salvation; that is the notion that a person can save another person or that a person can pay the debt of others. Islam teaches that every person is responsible for his/her own misdeeds. Islam, therefore, rejects the teaching of Christianity that Jesus of Nazareth is the savior of the world. Salvation is personal.

> *"But for those who believe and do good deeds there will be Gardens graced with flowing streams: that is the great triumph."* **Quran 85:11(Abdel Haleem)**

Despite the belief within Judaism of vicarious blessings and curses, the Jewish prophet Ezekiel (Ezek. 33:15-16) concurred with the Qur'an that individuals will be saved or damned by their individual deeds. The Qur'an cites salvific benefits to the performance of good deeds, but the benefits are not vicarious. Good deeds save only the person that does the good deeds. Like the Epistle of James (2:18) in the Christian Canon of Scriptures, Islam prioritizes deeds. Jesus was a man of action. He fed the hungry and healed the sick. The Qur'an usually associates faith and good deeds:

> *The truly good are those who believe in God and the Last Day, in the angels, the Scripture, and the prophets; who give away some of their wealth, however much they cherish it, to their relatives, orphans, the needy, the traveler, and beggars, and to liberate those in bondage; those who keep up the prayer and pay the prescribed alms; who keep pledges whenever they make them; who are steadfast in misfortune, adversity, and times of danger:it is they who are aware of God.*[xvii] **Surah 2:177**

Similarly, Islam concurs with Galatians 6:5 that every man must bear his own burden:

> *"Say, 'should I seek a Lord other than God, when He is the Lord of all things?' Each soul is responsible for its own actions: no soul will bear the burden of another. In the end, you will all return to your Lord and He will tell you the truth about your differences.* **Surah 6:164 (Abdel Haleem)**

Mecca was the original base of the religious activities of Mohammad. The Meccans had persecuted Mohammad and his followers for their uncompromising monotheism, their preaching and practice of social and racial equality--including raising the hopes of the poor--and against practices of the Arab Quraysh merchants, which Mohammad referred to as unethical. The Quraysh had accused him of threatening the social order of the city. His message was essentially the virtues of **Jesus Christ.** Mohammad and his followers admired the virtues of Jesus. Not surprisingly, he (Mohammad) sent some of his followers to Abyssinia with hope to establish a security alliance with its Christian Emperor.[cviii]

Muhammad fled from Mecca to Yathrib, (current city of Medina) in 622 C.E. shortly after a Muslim community was formed there in Yathrib. The Islamic Community at Yathrib welcomed Mohammad and his fellow Meccan exiles with jubilant hymn singing. That hijra, or migration, was the turning point in the life of Mohammad and Islam. The Islamic calendar begins with the hijra to Yathrib (Medina). Islam espouses the virtues of faith in God, submission to God, and right actions as the bridges to salvation.

The city of Yathrib (Medina) was a plural society of Jews, Muslims, and others, which may have included some Nestorian Christians living together harmoniously when Mohammad and his fellow Muslims from Mecca got there. All signed off on the **"Charter of Medina,"** which recognized and allowed religious autonomy to Jews, Muslims, and others. All residents of Yathrib comprised *one* *unitive community, and all were* obligated to contribute to the defense of the city against external threats. Although the city's plurality was complicated with the inclusion of three separate Jewish tribes, the community elected Muhammad to be its political leader.

Although Mohammad apparently related well with the Jewish tribes in Medina, he found one tribe to be most clannish and difficult to control. He said that God revealed to him that Jews were the most hostile tribe against Islam, and that Christians were the nearest in love to them.[cix] That probably explains the near extinction of one Jewish tribe in Medina. Despite disagreements, the Jews were not exiled or forced to convert to Islam. They were only forced to pay tribute.

It is apparent that Jesus is whatever and whoever the religious communities want Him to be and said that He was. The Gnostic tended to give Him the persona of a phantom. Islam, in its effort to show an apparent error of Christianity, put Him in the witness box of an assimilated court and made Him testify against His divinity. God was the president of the inquest. The Qur'an makes this comment:

> *"When God says, 'Jesus son of Mary, did you say to people, 'Take me and my mother as two gods alongside God?' he will say, 'may you be exalted! I would never say what I had no right to say – if I had said any such thing You would have known it. You know all that is within me, though I do*

not know what is within you. You alone have full knowledge of things unseen. I told them only what you commanded me to: 'Worship God, my Lord and your Lord.'" **Surah 5:116-118 (Abdel Haleem)**

GOD EMPTIED "SELF" INTO A MAN

17

NATIVITY OF JESUS IN THE QUR'AN

The nativity of Jesus in the Qur'an is similar to that in the Gospels according to Matthew and Luke of the Christian Canon. The angel Gabriel apparently spooked Mary. She was not accustomed to have a male visitor in her bedroom. She panicked and apparently screamed:

> *"I seek the Lord of Mercy's protection against you:*
> *if you have any fear of Him [do not approach!]"*
> *(Abdel Haleem)* - **Surah 19:18**

The angel Gabriel was obviously a male. All angels in the Judeo-Christian Bible are males. The reason is obvious. That was additional trauma for Maryam. Had the neighbors seen her male visitor she would have been morally compromised. Gabriel did his best to assure her of his innocence as a messenger from God,

> *"I am but a Messenger from your Lord, [come] to*
> *announce to you the gift of A pure son."*
> *(Abdel Haleem)* - **Surah 19.19**

Gabriel's response was not very reassuring. It elicited another quizzical response from Mary;

"How can I have a son when no man has touched me, I have not been unchaste?"
Surah 19.20 (Abdel Haleem)

It is apparent that the emotional climate was evolving from that of panic to one of uneasy calm; calm enough for a normal conversation. Maryam may have been musing that should Gabriel be telling the truth; the reason of his visit may be to judge and punish her. Gabriel then said to her:

"This is what your Lord said: 'It is easy for Me – We shall make him a sign to all people, a blessing from Us." (Abdel Haleem) - **Surah 19.21**

The Lucan story of the annunciation to Mary (Luke 1:29-34) is like that of the Qur'an which is:

"The angel said to Mary: 'Mary, God has chosen you and make you pure: He has truly chosen you above all women. Mary, be devoted to your Lord, prostrate yourself in worship, bow down with those who pray. ... Mary, God gives you news of a Word from Him, whose name will be the Messiah, Jesus, son of Mary, who will be held in honor in this world and the next, who will be one of those brought near to God. He will speak to people in his infancy and in his adulthood. He will be one of the righteous."
Surah 3:42-43, 45-46

There are three recorded ways of how a child is conceived and born. The first is that of having a father without a mother. That was the stories of divine creation in the book of Genesis (1:27 & 2:7). The second is the norm for the procreation of human being; the cohabitation of male and female. The third is that of a woman without a man; the stories of the nativity of Jesus Christ of Nazareth in the Gospels according to Matthew (18-21) and Luke (1:26-35) and the Qur'an (Surah 3:42-46). The pregnancy of an unwed woman is stressful to that woman, and that stress becomes draconian when the negative opinions and gossips of neighbors are added. Mary was still a virtuous virgin when a messenger told her that God planned to make her the mother of a special child. Because the annunciation was made to her and not publicly in a Temple, she faced naysayers when she attempted to explain how she became pregnant. Her options were limited. What could she do?

"She ... withdrew to a distant place."
Surah 19.22 (Abdel Haleem)

The far place is apparently in the Arabian Desert. The Qur'an sent a mixed message about the support of here parents. It suggests that they accompanied her to the far place, and that she went to the far place alone. She could have relocated to an aunt or even a distant relative to conceal the apparent shame. She obviously retreated to a distant oasis away from the prying eyes of villagers.

> *"She withdrew from her family to a place east and secluded herself away; we sent our spirit to appear before her in the form of a normal human."*
> **Surah 19:16-17 (Abdel Haleem)**

Mary was obviously a modest young woman. She and her nuclear family was concerned about the community's perception of her sexual morality. The annunciation, like the annunciation in the Gospel according to Luke (1:26 & 27), was done by a male human being. Angel are invariably male. The reasons may be legion, but one reason is that it was socially improper for women messengers to go on missions unaccompanied by a related male escort. The Qur'anic annunciation to Maryam is like that of the annunciation to Mary in the Gospel according to Luke. Mary was apparently confused. The Qur'an expressed the painful scenario graphically:

> *"When the pain of childbirth drove her to [cling to] the trunk of a palm tree, she exclaimed, 'I wish I had been dead and forgotten long before this."*
> *(Abdel Haleem)* - **Surah 19.23**

At birth, Jesus knew and understood the fragile emotions of His mother and sought to comfort her. He assured her that God had prepared for her needs.

> *"But a voice cried to her from below, 'Do not worry: Your Lord has provided a stream at your feet and, if you shake the trunk of the palm tree towards you,*

it will deliver fresh ripe dates for you. So eat, drink, be glad." (Abdel Haleem) - **Surah 19.24 -26A**

Jesus was the public face of his mother, Mary. He apparently sought to shield her from the embarrassment of explaining her pregnancy and His birth. He advised her:

"And say to anyone you see: I have vowed to the Lord of Mercy to abstain from conversation, and I will not talk to anyone today" (Abdel Haleem)
Surah 19:26

Maryam's draconian social pain seemed to drag on forever. Her parents and their social associates may have doubted the story she told about the conception of the child. The Qur'an detailed the tongue lashings:

"She went back to her people carrying the child, and they said, 'Mary! You have done something terrible! Sister of Aaron! Your father was not a bad man; your mother was not unchaste."
Surah 19:27 -28

Mary hoped that Jesus would convince them of the sincerity of what she had told them.

"She pointed at him. They said, 'How can we converse with an infant?... He said, 'I am a servant of God. He has granted me the Scriptures; made me a prophet; made me blessed wherever I

> *may be. He commanded me to pray, to give alms
> as long as I live, to cherish my mother. He did not
> make me domineering or graceless. Peace be on
> me the day I was born, and will be on me the day I
> die, and the day I am raised to life again. Such was
> Jesus, Son of Mary."*
> **Surah 19:27-34 (Abdel Haleem)**

Contrary to what Christianity teaches about the nativity or birth of Jesus of Nazareth, Islam and the Qur'an does not refer to the Holy Spirit as the mean or medium of Mary's conception. It said simply that Mary became pregnant while still being chaste and a virgin. Islam teaches that an angel or a messenger of God conferred the Holy Spirit on Jesus. It is like one of the heresies of Christianity-- adoptionism. The Qur'an names the conferring of the Holy Spirit on Jesus His confirmation as a prophet:

> *"Certainly, we gave Moses the Book, and followed
> him with the apostles, and we gave Jesus, son of
> Mary, manifest proof, and confirmed him with Thy
> Holy Spirit."* - **Surah 2:87**

The Qur'an refers to Jesus as a prophet of God and His miracles were done only as God permitted. The following is addressed to Jesus to emphasize His servanthood to God.

> *"Then God will say, "Jesus, Son of Mary!
> Remember my favor to you and to your Mother:
> how I strengthen you with the Holy Spirit, so*

> *that you spoke to people in your infancy and as a grown man; how I taught you in the Scripture and wisdom, the Torah and the Gospel; how, by my leave, you fashioned the shape of a bird out of clay, breathed into it, and it became, by My leave, a bird; how, by my leave you healed the blind person and the leper; how, by my leave, you brought the dead back to life; . . . When the disciples said, 'Jesus, son of Mary, can your Lord send down a feast for us from heaven. ... Jesus, son of Mary, said, 'Lord, send down to us a feast from heaven. ... You are the best provider."* - **Surah 5.110-114**

Although the nativity stories of Jesus of Nazareth seem alike in the Scriptures of Christianity (New Testament) and Islam (Qur'an), there are major differences between them. Christianity, according to Tertullian the North African, said that God "slid into the womb of Mary." Islam denies that the baby in Mary's womb was divine. Islam, however, like Byzantine Christianity, credits Jesus with having adult faculties even when he was an infant. The similarities end there.

Even when Christians and Muslims use similar phrases, the phrases often mean something different. The prologue of the Gospel according to John, for example, imply the incarnation of God as human to Christians. Islam interprets it (Word of God) only as a reference to the providence of God.[cx]

Islam denounces and rejects all fabrication of images that depict divinity whether they be human or beasts. They suspect all images of leading to idolatry. Islam's avoidance of images, a doctrine known as "Aniconism" places a road block to meaningful dialogue of Christians and Muslims. Islam frowns on the making and use of icons.

> *"He who makes an image will be punished by God on the Day of the Resurrection until he breathes life into it – which he will not be able to do."*[xxi]

The Qur'an was written almost six hundred years after the nativity of Jesus of Nazareth and John the Baptist. Muhammad probably knew about Jesus Christ and understood contemporary Christology, probably the Christology of Nestorians. He did not believe that Jesus was divine, that He was crucified, or that He rose from the dead. Stephen Prothero, in *God is not One*, said that Islam and Christianity are selectively inclined to Judaism: Islam inclines to the Orthopraxy or right action of Judaism, and Christianity to the orthodoxy, or right doctrine of Judaism.

See also this invective against the idea of a son of God (Allah).

> *"It befits not the majesty of Allah that He should beget a son. Glorified is He above all that they associate with Him. When He decrees a thing, He says to it 'Be' and it is."* - **Surah 19:30-35**

18

JESUS OF NAZARETH: THE PROPHET OF ISLAM

Contrary to the perception of many Christians, there are many references to Jesus of Nazareth in the Qur'an-- twenty-five to be exact. The name Jesus is mentioned more often than the name of the prophet Mohammad. Amad is one of the names for Jesus of Nazareth in the Qur'an. It is an Arabic word which means "highly praised." His mother, Mary or Maryam, is the only woman that is named in the Qur'an. An entire chapter, or Surah, is dedicated to her coverage. Name count of the names Jesus and Mohammad is not a benchmark by which to rate their relative importance. Mohammad is the major prophet of Islam, and his importance is not determined by the number of references to him by name. A Christian pastor in Florida erred when he critiqued the prayer of a colleague at a civic function in Jacksonville, Florida, based on the number of times he referred to Jesus by name. Quantity is less important than relevance. Muslims believe that God revealed the contents of the Qur'an to Mohammad and that Jesus of Nazareth is the living Torah to Christians, and a prophet second in importance only to Mohammad for Islam.

In spite of the fact that Islam acknowledges Jesus only as a prophet and the Messiah, and not as the Son of God or God in flesh (incarnate) as the Scriptures of Christianity said he is, it teaches that God prepared Maryam to be the mother of Jesus the Messiah in response to the prayer of her parents, Hannah and Imran. Maryam and Samuel, the prophet of Judaism, have much in common.

The Qur'an said that Jesus was immaculately conceived and birthed. As mentioned elsewhere, Islam teaches that all conceptions and birth are immaculate (without sin). Islam also teaches that Maryam conceived when she was still a virgin. She is mentioned more times in the Qur'an than she is mentioned in the Christian New Testament.

When Mohammad defeated the Quraysh of Mecca in 630 C.E., he destroyed all the idols in Mecca except that of Maryam and Jesus.[cxii] The Quran suggests that Jesus of Nazareth was sent to lead a peace movement. The infant Jesus reportedly said:

> *"He did not make me domineering or graceless.*
> *Peace was on me the day I was born and will be*
> *on me the day I die and the day I am raised to life*
> *again."* - **Surah 19:30-34 (Abdel Haleem)**

The clause, "*I am a servant of God*" defines His role as an Islamic prophet.

JESUS OF NAZARETH: THE PROPHET OF ISLAM

"The angel said, 'Maryam, God gives you news of a Word from him, whose name will be the Messiah, Jesus, son of Maryam, who will be held in honor in this world and the next, . . . He will speak to people in his infancy and in his adulthood."

- (Surah 3, ayat 45)

Although Christianity teaches that Jesus is the final revelation of God to human beings, it does not deny that Mohammad was a prophet. Mohammad also said that Jesus was a Muslim. He said the same about the patriarchs of Judaism. Christian theologian Hans Kung suggests that Muhammad's version of Christianity may have been the Christianity of the early converts to Christianity from Judaism. Some of that group of Christians, known as Ebionites, survived in regions to the East of Palestine and probably in Arabia. They were not Hellenized by the Christian councils. The Ebionites regarded Jesus of Nazareth as the Messiah but denied his divinity. They used the Gospel according to Matthew, but only a version that begins at the 3rd chapter. They dismissed the apostle Paul as an apostate of the Torah and distanced themselves from the Temple priests, who they believed were corrupt. They highly valued optional poverty, sabbath keeping, circumcision, and the Temple liturgy.

Waraqa bin Naufal, a cousin of Mohammad by marriage and an Ebionite Christian who read the Gospel in Arabic, made Mohammad aware that the revelations he was receiving was like that of Moses.[cxiii] Muhammad was apparently well versed in the polytheism of Arabia and

Ebionite, and probably Nestorian Christianity. The phrase "Son of god" which referred to sons of El was anathema to him.

In Christian Christology, Jesus is the "Word of God that becomes flesh" (John 1:1 & 14), but Islam designates him a servant or slave of God. Jesus of Christianity is really Lord as well as servant. Islam does not teach that Jesus ought to be believed in as Lord or that He was crucified, died, rose from death, and ascended to heaven. It teaches that the body of Jesus was assumed into heaven and that Jesus will be honored forever. Although the Qur'an does not have any reference to the resurrection of Jesus, it does refer to the resurrection of the believers:

> *"God does not guide those who misguide [others], nor will they have anyone to guide them. They have sworn by God with their strongest hopes that He will not raise the dead to life. But He will – it is His binding promise, though most people do not believe it . . . the disbelievers may realize that that what they said is false."* - **Surah 16:37-39 (Abdel Haleem)**

Jesus is the messenger and prophet of God. He is a man calling them to be faithful to God and to help Him in the ministry of evangelism. The Qur'an teaches that Jesus is an active Muslim.

> *"When Jesus became aware that they [still] did not believe, he said, 'Who will help me in God's cause?'*

The disciples said, 'We will be God's helpers; we believe in God – witness our devotion to Him."
Surah 3:52-53

The comment of the disciples is interesting. It suggests a fraternal relationship with Jesus. It is a "We too" statement:

"We are God's helpers"

The people who were with Jesus bore witness to his miraculous power. They believed that his miracles were done only as God permitted him to do them.

"I have brought you a Sign from your Lord. I will create the shape of a bird out of the clay for you and then breathe into it, and it will be a bird by God's permission. I will tell you what you eat and what you store up in your homes . . . heal the blind and the leper and bring the dead to life, by God's permission." - **Surah 3:49**

There is also the suggestion that whatever man can do; God can do it better.

"The [disbelievers] scheme but God also schemed; God is the Best of Schemers."

Jesus is meant to be a leader as well as a prophet. Judgment belongs to God, and God will judge more favorably those who listen to the message of Jesus and follow him.

> *"God said, 'Jesus, I will take you back and raise you up to Me; I will purify you of the disbelievers. To the Day of Resurrection, I will make those who followed you superior to those who disbelieved. Then you will return to Me and I will judge between you regarding your differences."*
> - **Surah 3:55**

Both Christianity and Islam prioritize right action. Jesus, in the Lord's Prayer in the Gospels according to Matthew (Matt. 6:9-13) and Luke (Luke 11:2-4), emphasizes forgiveness. The Islamic Version of that prayer is:

> *"Our Lord! Condemn us not if we forget or miss our mark! . . . Pardon us, absolve us, have mercy on us, Thou our protector. And give us victory over disbelieving folks. Show us the straight path. The path of those whom Thou hast favored; not (the path) of those who earn Thine anger nor of those who go astray."* - **Surah 2:286**

The Qur'an links people who accept the revelations of God with access to the garden. That garden is apparently the new Eden or paradise. The Gospel according to Matthew and Mark of the Christian Canon linked wealth and the difficulty to enter the kingdom of God, but Islam links it to receiving the revelations.

The Qur'an reads:
"The gates of heaven will not be open to those who rejected our revelations and arrogantly spurn them, even if a thick rope were to pass through the eye of a needle they would not enter the Garden. This is how we punish the guilty." - **Surah 7:40**

The version of that saying in the synoptic Gospels of Christianity (Matt. 19:24; Mark 10:25; Luke 18:25) reads:

"It will be easier for a camel to pass through the eye of a needle than for a rich man to enter the Kingdom of Heaven." **(Living Bible Version)**

The New Testament Scriptures and the Qur'an may have had in mind the "Needle Eye" gate in the wall around the city of Jerusalem, but it could also be meant literally. Both the Gospels of the Christian canon and the Qur'an make a connection with the "gates of heaven" and a camel going through the Needle's Eye gate, or it may literally mean the eye of a needle. The Quran put the emphasis on acceptance of the revelations that God gave.

The Qur'an associates Abraham, Ishmael, Isaac, Jacob, the Tribes, Moses, and Jesus. They are the de facto family of God, and God does not favor one over another. The following is a divine endorsement of the lineage:

"We believe in what has been given to Moses, Jesus, and the prophets from their Lord. We do not make a distinction between any of them. It is to Him that

we devote our- selves.' If anyone seeks a religion other than [Islam] complete devotion to God, it will not be accepted from Him: he will be one of the losers in the Hereafter." - **Surah 3:84-85**

Sayyid Gesus Daraz, a member of the Indian Muslim Chishti Tariqa, recounts a mysterious vision he had. One must, of course, be always mindful of the nature of visions and dreams and how they reveal what is in the subconscious. They may not reveal anything new but bring us face to face with our anxieties and subconscious desires. Daraz's vision was that he was wading waist-deep in a lake, in which there was a girl of about fifteen years of age. The girl beckoned to him and a conversation developed. He and the girl claimed to be a parent of Jesus. Jesus denied that He was the son of either of them but was the "Son of God." The dream of Daraz is probably a subliminal reflection of the Muslim Chishti Tariqa people. The commentary on the vision continued:

"A man from the world of the unknown was a witness to this. He threw a cloak over us as though to hide us, and at that moment I saw myself clothed in the same beauty and grace as she. From between us the prophet Jesus arose and cried out, 'I am the Son of God'. The two of us began to quarrel, I am saying that Jesus was my child and she is saying, 'No he is mine' . . . Settling the dispute, Jesus said, "I am neither your son nor hers . . . I am only of

> *and with myself.*[xxiv] *Jesus' response to Daraz and the verbal tug-of-war between him and the girl does not express a typical Islamic Christology or doctrine of Jesus Christ. "Son of God" is Christian Christology. It is not clear what Daraz meant when he said, "The prophet Jesus rose and cried out, 'I am the Son of God." That is interesting. In Islamic thought, Jesus would be addressed as prophet or referred to as the Messiah. It is Jesus, however, who referred to himself as the "Son of God." The Chishti Tariqa community is probably a religious syncretism of Christianity and Islam. The other possibility is that Jesus, who is above all faith communities, makes pronouncements that are outside of sectarian restraints.*

The Qur'an identifies Jesus of Nazareth as the Islamic prophet that reprimands Torah apostates. The apostates to which it makes reference are probably contemporaries of Jesus. It may also refer to Jews and Christians along the trajectory of Judeo-Christian salvation history. Daraz may have been seeing Jesus as the "New Torah," because He is the new Divine Canon or God's Standard to measure excellence.

The Qur'an uses the voice of Jesus of Nazareth to deny His divinity against the Christian apologist who proclaimed Him to be Lord. He denounces those who worship Him as God. The indictment begins with an introductory statement followed by a question:

> *"Those who say, 'God is the Messiah, son of Mary,' have defied God. The Messiah himself said, 'Children of Israel, worship God, my Lord and your Lord.' If anyone associates others with God, God will forbid him from the Garden, and Hell will be his home. No one will help [such] evildoers."*
> **Surah 5:72**

According to Islam, putting God on the same level with the Messiah is to debase God. For God to be debased and become a creature is repulsive to Judaism and Islam. God is wholly spiritual and mankind is material. That the spiritual and the material are wholly separate and apart is a criterion of Islam. There are also moral implications associated with the idea of humans procreating with God or gods. It sounds pagan and is disturbing to Muslim religious sensitivity.

19

JESUS OF NAZARETH IN CHRISTIANITY AND ISLAM: DIFFERENCES AND SIMILARITIES

Pierre Teilhard de Chardin wrote in *How I Believe,* "We have without any doubt been watching for the last century the birth and establishment of a new faith, the religion of evolution." Everything evolves. Christianity, if you are a Christian, may be a higher level of faith and worship over Judaism. If you are a Muslim, you will say that Islam is a step above Christianity. The truth is that Judaism, Christianity, and Islam are religions that have been revealed to human beings by God. Islam and Judaism are simple monotheistic religions and Christianity may have evolved to become the most complex monotheism. That complex monotheism has been vigorously critiqued by some Christians as well as Jews and Muslims. It is the end product of much conflict and debates at councils of religious and secular participants. Muslims and Jews reject the Trinitarianism of Christianity. The Qur'an opines:

> *"The Jews said, 'Ezra is the son of God,' and
> Christians said, 'the Messiah is the son of God'...
> They take their rabbis and their monks as lords
> beside God, as well Christ, the son of Mary. But
> they were commanded to serve only one God; there is
> no god but Him; He is far above whatever they set
> up as His partners!"*
>
> - Surah 9:30-31 (Abdel Haleem)

The "Him" referred to in the Qur'an may be Yahweh- Elohim, El Roi, El Shaddai of Judaism and Allah together. There are many names for God, but they refer or point to one God, which Pierre de Chardin suggests is the One God of every faith community. Although there is the concept of the ninety-nine names of God (Allah) of Islam, Muslims believe in One God. The many names are manifestations of that One God. Jews know God as YHWH, Elohim, El Shaddai, El Roi, but the names are of the One God.

Jews, Christians, and Muslims affirm that there is only one God." When Jews read the Torah in the Temple, they enunciated "Adonai" wherever the Torah text has the name YHWH. They never think of two gods when they see the word YHWH and enunciate "Adonai." They substitute Adonai for YHWH because of their deference to holiness of the name YHWH. Allah may have been used instead of "Adonai."[cxv] Allah is and has been the name of God in Syria and among other Arabic speaking people even before the rise of Islam. Christians and Animists refer to God as Allah in some areas in the Middle East before the rise of

Islam. It was both a common name for god and the name of a special God.

The English word "God" refers to that which is worshipped. Anselm of Canterbury defined God as, "*That than which nothing can be greater.*" That One God revealed the name (YHWH) Yahweh or Jahweh to Moses. YHWH became the God of Israel. Jews, Christians, and Muslims acknowledge YHWH as that One God. Christianity differs from Judaism and Islam with its confessional dogma that the one God was incarnate as a human being. Whatever one chose to call that one God, Christians believe his is incarnate as Jesus of Nazareth. Jesus is Islam's prophet, as well as Messiah and Christ, but not God. Therein lies the great difference between Christianity and Islam.

Although Islam rejects the divinity of Jesus, it teaches that he, the son of Maryam (Mary) is their pen-ultimate prophet of God.

GOD EMPTIED "SELF" INTO A MAN

20

ISLAMIC PERSPECTIVE: WHO KILLED JESUS?

The Qur'an does not mention the crucifixion of Jesus. Islam does not teach that he was crucified at Golgotha. He may have had a premonition that the Jews would kill him, and he frustrated their plan. The Gospels according to Matthew and Luke (Christian Canon) implied that premonition:

> *"Jerusalem! Jerusalem! you kill the prophets, stoned the messengers God has sent you!"*
> **(Luke 13:34)**

The Matthean Text was probably written after the destruction of the Temple in Jerusalem and may not have been a prophecy. It reads:

> *'Jerusalem, Jerusalem! You kill the prophets and stone the messengers God has sent you! . . . . And so*

your Temple will be abandoned and empty."
Matt. 23:37–38 (GNB-TEV)

Jesus' indictment of the people of Jerusalem is the perennial indictment for not following the teachings of the Torah. The Qur'an and Islamic commentators suggest that although they boasted that they killed Jesus, they did not-- because He did not die on the cross. The Qur'an suggests that the Jews falsely claimed to have crucified Jesus and will bear the consequence of that boast.

> *"And because they disbelieved and uttered a terrible slander against Mary, and said, 'We have killed the Messiah, Jesus son of Mary, the messenger of God'. (They did not kill him, nor did they crucify him, though it was made to appear like that to them; . . . There is not one of the people of the Book who will not believe in (Jesus) before the death, and on the Day of Resurrection he shall stand as a witness against them."* - **Surah 4:156-159 (Abdel Haleem)**

The Qur'an suggests that Jesus was misunderstood by many of the people of the Book. The Canonical Gospels of Christianity also suggested that Jesus was misunderstood. Jesus also implied in the Canonical Gospels of Christianity that many who followed Him did so because of the material benefits He offered and provided. They were interested only in material benefits. Some were attracted to Him because He gave them dinner for gratis.

"Ye seek me, not because you saw the miracles, but because ye did eat of the loaves, and were filled."
1 John 6:26 (KJAV)

The Qur'an denied that Jesus was crucified and implied that whatever happened was done in accord with the will of God, who controls all processes. It is not clear what the Qur'an means by, "Ever since you took my soul" and "it is not you who killed me," since it denied that Jesus died at the scene and time of the supposed crucifixion. It may be a reference to the ascension into heaven of the living body of Jesus. It could be a reference to suggestions that the Jews knew that they did not kill Him. Muslims suggest that Simon of Cyrene or a renegade Roman soldier was the victim of the cross. Their theory of what happened at the scene of the supposed crucifixion may have been influenced by the gnostic gospel, according to Basilides.[cxvi] The Qur'an suggests that Jesus ascended to the uncreated Father;

"God raised him up unto Himself."
Surah 4, ayat 158 (Abdel Haleem)

The gnostic version of what happened at Golgotha is that God took Jesus alive, active or sleeping, into heaven. This is consistent with the ascension of Jesus (Acts 1:9-11, Christian Canon) and the ascension of Enoch.

Genesis 5:24 (KJV).
"Enoch walked with God: and he was not; for God took him."

Walking with God implies having a close relationship with God. Jews, Christians, and Muslims aspired to that quality relationship with God (YHWH). Enoch had a relationship with God, which replicates life before sin. The fall alienated man from God. Walking with God is consistent with another dogma of the Western Church; that dogma that Mary the Mother of Jesus slept (Dormition) and was taken up alive to heaven.

Christians teach that Jesus ascended into heaven forty days after the Easter Moment. Although Muslims deny His death on the cross and His resurrection to life on the first day of the week, they believe that He was taken up to heaven on the day of the supposed crucifixion. A passage in the Qur'an suggests that Simon of Cyrene or a Roman soldier may have been crucified in the place of Jesus of Nazareth at Golgotha. Although that implies divine deception, it is nonetheless an interesting idea. Simon of Cyrene walked with Jesus (God) and Enoch walked with YHWH (God). They were both lifted up. One lifted up on a cross; the other lifted into the celestial abode of God.

21

THE FUTURE OF JESUS CHRIST IN ISLAM

Jesus, Son of Mary, is a person without which there would be no Islam. Muslims adore the Lord of Christianity, but only as a prophet and Messiah, or anointed one, Christ. They do not acknowledge him as their Lord and savior, or the savior of mankind. Although Jesus of Nazareth is very important to Christians and Muslims, each understand him differently. Despite the different perspectives of Islam and Christianity on Jesus of Nazareth, neither can rationally deny his role in the development of the two faith communities.

Many Christians and many Muslims identify with Christianity and Islam only as cultures. Some of them associate religion with nationality. Some Christians have a Bible in one hand and a national flag in the other. Muslims do likewise; a Qur'an in one hand and the national flag in the other. Christians believe that Jesus is their Lord, and Muslims believe that he is their prophet - the prophet to whom God was most fully revealed. That said, Christians and Muslims should be living peacefully as neighbors. That, however, is easier said than done. Imams who radicalize their congregations downplay the role of Jesus in Islam, and some Christian pastors demonize Muslims. Few Christians know that there is multiple reference to Jesus and his mother in the Qur'an, or that Jesus of Nazareth is adored, but not worshipped, by Muslims.

Given the geopolitical biases and the coopting of religious cults to energize partisans, Jesus is openly embraced by Christians and apparently depressed by radicalizing imams to hype their cults' identity. There is no sign that the mutual hostility between Jews, Christians, and Muslims is abating despite the interdependence made necessary by global trade and commerce. Islam has replaced Communism as the ideology to malign in the West where many people believe that Islam is a cult of violence that encourages and glorifies suicide. Although I have not met and interacted with many Muslims, my reading of the Qur'an suggests to me that Christianity and Islam have an affinity that can be harnessed for peace-making. Some Christians and some Muslims, and Jews, however, feel that the name Jesus of Nazareth is a non-starter for peace dialog.

I learned that, when I volunteered to help plan an interfaith-interracial Ecumenical Peace Liturgy for the faith communities on the far South-side of Chicago for Thanksgiving Day in 1979. Invitations went out to Christian pastors, Jewish rabbis, and Muslim imams. The response was very encouraging. There were many jaundiced eyes crisscrossing the room during the initial planning session. Despite the apprehension of many, Jews,

Christians, and Muslims gathered under the welcoming roof of a Christian Church. There were only two tense moments; one being the characterization of a Christian pastor by a Muslim as "a white devil." The other being a sharp question for clarification of Trinitarianism by a member of a Pentecostal Church. Because the stated purpose was "peace-making," we pushed forward without debate. There was no reference in the prayers that they were offered through Jesus Christ. That was done in deference to the participating rabbis. Christian participants did not know that Muslims know about Jesus, and we developed a common liturgy without having a clue about what Muslims believe. None of the Christian pastors, including me, had ever read the Qur'an.

In my reading, praying, and thinking I can see Jesus Christ, the man from Nazareth, calling and giving words of wisdom to Jews, Christians, and Muslims alike. Judaism sees God most clearly in the Torah, Christianity sees God Jesus Christ, and Islam see God as revealed to them through the prophets-- especially Jesus of Nazareth and Mohammad. I feel obliged to pass on the advice of the first theologian of Christianity, Paul of Tarsus, who in a letter to the Christians in Rome said:

> *"Welcome those who are weak in faith, but do not argue with them about their personal opinions."*
> **Rom. 14:1 (GND-TEV)**

I would not characterize Islam as a religion that is weak in faith. I would however suggest that to believe that Jesus died and rose from the dead, ascended, and returned as the Holy Spirit, makes Christianity a religion of extreme strong faith. Someone with those characteristics is all over the Judeo-Christian Bible. The 11th chapter of the Book of Revelations (1-14) has a reference to an end of the age struggle between the forces of good and evil which Ulrich Wilckens[cxvii] suggests may be a reference to the resurrection of Moses and Elijah to fight the Lord's battle. The resurrection of Jesus Christ may point to his perpetual presence on earth and in heaven. (Psalm 110:1)

Jesus is a kinsman of Abraham, and Christianity declared that he is divine. Jews, Christians, and Muslims cherish the kinship of Abraham (Gen. 17:7-10). Some probably believe that the kinship is a bloodline which may be a connection which can be traced by DNA. The ancestry, however, may be spiritual and not physical. Jews may seek to trace their ancestry to Abraham by way of Moses, Jacob, and Isaac; Muslims may try to do likewise through Ishmael and Hagar.

Jews, Christians, and Muslims may be connected to Abraham spiritually and not genetically. The fallacy of misreading texts has implications for war and peace. It is my understanding that the uniqueness of Judaism, Christianity, and Islam is mode of revelations and not ethnicity. The difference between ethnic and faith connectivity is as follows:

1. Ethnicity.
    a.   The Jewish ancestry is traced to Abraham and Sarah through Moses and Jacob.

b. Muslims (initially Arabs) ancestry is traced to Abraham and Hagar through Ishmael.

2. Mode of Revelation.

a. God revealed "Himself" and the Torah to the Hebrews through Moses. Many of those Hebrews were not genetically related (Judaism).
b. God is revealed in Jesus, the son of Mary. The Church is a gathering of strangers (Christianity).
c. God reveals the kitab (Qur'an) to Mohammad. Islam may be initially the faith of Arab clansmen but became a multi-ethnic religion (Islam).

A comment attributed to Jesus in the Qur'an confirms His mode of revelation.

> *"Children of Israel, I am sent to you by God confirming the Torah that came before me and bringing good news of a messenger to follow me whose name will be Ahmad."*[xxviii] **- Surah 61:6**

Ahmad is a name of the prophet Mohammad. It means "Much praised." God fully revealed the Kitab (Book) to the Prophet Mohammad (Islam).

Christianity and Islam are faithful to the book; the Bible and the Qur.an. The name of Jesus as Lord and as prophet is everywhere in those two books. He is by implication YHWH incarnate to Christians and is the prophet of Allah to Muslims. Social media has made Jesus more than the cult personality of Christianity. He is a major figure in comparative religious and philosophical studies in grade schools, and colleges, and even non-Christian seminaries. Several secular colleges and universities offer course in "Bible as literature" and the Wisdom of Jesus. He referred to himself as Truth when the Roman procurator of Judea, Pilate, asked the question, "Are you are a king, then?" He responded:

> *"I was born and came into the world for this one purpose, to speak about the truth. Whoever listens to the truth listens to me."* **John 18:37 (GNB- TEV)**

Jesus made himself the symbol of truth telling. My maternal grandmother who always modeled Jesus to me, always demanded that I speak the truth. She confessed to having been contaminated by the ethics of her environment, but told me with tightly curled lips and a frown that betrayed much anxiety and stress:

> *"Lying is an abomination unto the Lord even if it helps in time of trouble."*

Jesus' relevance and influence swings like a pendulum. Although Judaism denied that he could be a Jewish prophet, several Jewish seminaries teach courses on the Gospels of Christianity.

Jesus of Nazareth is an international cultural icon. The national motto of the USA, "In God We Trust" implied trust in Jesus Christ, and many associate Western civilization with Jesus of Nazareth. Many Jews in the Western hemisphere have moved outside of Jewish ghettos and exchange greetings with their Christian and Muslim neighbors who celebrate Christmas, Easter, Passover and Yom Kippur, and Ramadan as the new normal. The God-man of Christianity and the prophet and Christ of Islam may not have meant much to Jews, but he has become an international cultural icon.

Europe has a large Muslim minority population owing to:

a. The Arab-Islamic conquest of North Africa going into the Iberian Peninsula. (711-788 C.E.).

b. Islam's conquest of Turkey and the Turkish foray into the Balkans and parts of Central Europe in the fifteenth century.

c. Migration from Muslim majority countries that were colonized by European maritime nations during the Age of Discovery or were ruled under mandates of the League of Nations and the United Nations after the two World Wars.

Those who rule invariably feel that time is changeless. Given that mindset they rarely plan for change, but modern technology and mobility have built community despite the historic barriers and boundaries. Jesus of Nazareth is an invisible bridge in the creation of that community, and whoever wills to have power can achieve it with the available technology. Jesus of Nazareth is held up as the great advocate of peace, and many Christians keep alive the hope of the prophet Isaiah (Is. 2:4):

> *"He will settle disputes among great nations. They will hammer their swords into plows and their spears into pruning knives."*

Jesus obviously had that prophesy in mind when he told a disciple to sheathe his sword. People who feel that they are oppressed or had been oppressed peoples may reject the call for peace citing another statement of Jesus:

> *"Do not think that I have come to bring peace to the world. No. I did not come to bring peace, but a sword."* **Matthew 10:34-35 (GNB-TEV)**

Some Christians suggest that the above text reflects the Jesus of Islam. That is really the Jesus of Judaism, Christianity, and Islam. Jesus understood the human condition and spoke the truth about it. The name of Jesus will be heard in both war and peace. Some Muslims, some Jews, and some Christians are justifiably angry because they have experienced oppression at the hands of others because of the way they believe and worship the one God.

Oppression, real or perceived, drove some Jews, Christians, and Muslims to religious fundamentalism.

That is their security armor when they feel targeted for conversion to another faith community. North Americans who replace Europeans on the Christian mission fields may be numbed to the anxiety of Muslims who feel targeted for conversion, and Islamists who are concerned about Christian evangelism may be tempted to ignore Jesus in the Quran. As a smaller percentage of North Americans and western Europeans identify with cultic Christianity, the perceived connection of liberal capitalism with Christianity has boost the prospect for Christianity and Jesus among the less affluent, especially in the southern hemisphere. Islam has converted many African-American inmates who had been members of Christian churches. Jesus as prophet and philosopher is more easily understood than the concept of Jesus the god-man. At the same time, Jews have been chipping into the Christian majority through networking with Christians who are dissatisfied with their experiences in the Christian churches.

To rephrase a common thought of the 20th century, "If communism did not exist, the West would have to invent an adversary." Islam is the new adversary of the Christianized West. Raymond Baker refers to the revolution which began in Tahrir Square, Egypt, on January 25, 2011, as the "River of Life flowing."[cxix] Christians and Muslims have been partners in the liberating movement in Egypt. Christians feel empowered by Jesus as their Lord and Liberator, and Muslims have been motivated by Jesus as their Messiah and prophet. The river of life flows internationally. The hope is that more people will know that Jesus is a bridge between Christianity and Islam. Judaism has been pulled into that flowing "River of Life" by Evangelical Christians who see their salvation bound up with that of Israel and Jews, and Israel likewise knows that Evangelical Christianity is its greatest lobbyists outside of its synagogues.

POSTLUDE

Where do we go from here as Jews, Christians, and Muslims? Arab-Muslims and European Christians had exploited their less belligerent neighbors. Jews remember and celebrate their exiles and have studied and perfected the art of war and diplomacy as shields against the reoccurrence of past national injuries. Jews, Christians, and Muslims buoyed by memories of repression as well as the joys of their victories, initiate interfaith dialog to build alliances and develop relationships of trust. Religion, however, continues to be divisive. Many religious institutions continue to foster climates of exclusion to gain or maintain superiority.

When the Hebrews conquered and ethnically cleansed Palestine in the 12th century B.C.E., they did it because they believed that cohabitation could contaminate their religious purity. They believed that YHWH had elected them to be the priest-nation to the world. There is much that is conflictual. Priests are supposed to be bridges that connect people. Putting the Canaanites to the "ban" was a decision to eliminated them Did God require that punishment? Were slavery and serfdom required by God? Was the Nazis anti-Semitic pogrom in the plan of God? The aggressive response of Israel to terror attacks from the

Palestinian State on Israel may be defended as necessary national security measures. The demagoguery of militarily powerful Europeans may also be dismissed as the will of God. What people do in the name of God depends on their operand conditioning. Jews persecuted Christians when they could. Christians persecuted Jews when the balance of power changed. Arab Muslims raided their neighbors, including the Berbers along the North African coasts. They did likewise to Christians on the Iberian Peninsula and from the East into Central Europe.

European Christians and Arab Muslims were accomplices in the raids that harvested Black Africans for the lucrative Trans-Atlantic slave trade. They damaged Black African victims physically and emotionally by conditioning them to believe that a mythical ancestor, Ham, buggered his father Noah. That legitimized them as victims of the abusive institution of slavery. A retired African-American high school principal in a south-eastern USA state was convinced that his black skin and kinky hair symbolized divine punishment (Gen. 9:20-27) on Black Africans.

Socio-political religious hierarchs have unfortunately isolated and insulated people of faith to protect the orthodoxy of the faith. Some Muslims, especially those who are unaware of the multiple mention of Jesus in the Qur'an, are afraid to invoke the name of Jesus. Christians from the Middle East would be advised not to refer to God as "Allah" while visiting with Christian friends in Western Europe and North America. The image of Jesus of Nazareth has been damaged by the representation of him by unscrupulous Christians and Muslims.

Constantinian and post-Constantine Christendom has been maligned by many non-conformist Christian sects for its apparent complicity with, and dependence on the largesse of the Emperor. They accuse Orthodox Christianity of allowing Constantine to contaminate biblical Christianity. Although much of the critique of Constantinian Christendom is sectarian propaganda, there is unfortunately, the continuing human tendency to curry favor with the "Caesars" of this world to gain personal or group advantages over opponents. That was the norm in the fourth century of the Common Era going forward. Muslims and Jews have also depended on supportive military and political strongmen. Judah Cohen, writing about the organizational and liturgical conflicts among the Jews on the former Danish Virgin Island of St. Thomas, documented the power struggle between the Jewish sects on the island in the 19th century. Both sects sought the support of the King in Copenhagen and the legislators on the island for help to advance their sectarian aspirations.[cxx]

Despite the Reformation of Western Christianity in the 16th century and the sectarian wars of religion which were supported by emperors, kings, imperial electors, and the forces aligned with the Bishop of Rome, Christianity survived the carnage and prosper. Thanks to the support of monarchs and nobles who saw the potential of religion to stabilize the society. Christianity was also a collateral beneficiary of Europe's Age of Discovery.

Many Jews prospered in the many diaspora. They had an opportunity to return to Palestine after Jewish nationalist David Ben-Gurion unilaterally declared the independence of Israel in 1948. Ben-Gurion understood the collective guilt of Christian Europe for the Holocaust and knew a homeland in Palestine would be a suave to the pain of Nazi brutality, under which many Jews perished among the approximate 30 million victims of the Second World War.

Ben-Gurion enlisted in the British army's Jewish Legion despite the terrorization of Palestine by Turkish and British forces during the war. That enabled him to galvanize armed support for the declaration of independence of Israel on May 1948. Neither the United Kingdom, which held the mandate over Palestine, nor the United Nations registered any opposition to Ben Gurion's declaration of independence. He probably expected that response from the United Kingdom and felt that European and North American nominal Christians felt vicarious guilt with the nominal Christian people of Germany. Britain was probably overwhelmed by Jewish terrorists in Palestine.

Yawman-Nakbah, or the cataclysm of Palestinians, occurred the day after Israel declared its independence from the United Kingdom's United Nations Mandate. According to some estimates, more than 700,000 Arab Christians and Muslims were driven from their homes by the Israeli military. The critique of Yawman-Nakbah is not an indictment of Judaism. It is a comment on the human propensity to remember and revenge personal or group hurt.

Palestine was the stage on which God initiated and launched the development of Judaism, Christianity, and Islam and adherents of the three faiths return there on pilgrimages to reaffirm their heritage. Jesus of Nazareth is the Lord of Christianity and the church. The four evangelists: Matthew, Mark, Luke, and John tell us that Jesus trained 12 men to continue the ministry he began, The Gospel according to Matthew (16:13-20); Mark (8:27-30); Luke (9:18-20) refer to a conversation between Jesus and the 12 disciples while they were on retreat somewhere near the town of Caesarea Philippi. The Gospel according to Matthew goes into greater detail about the dialogue.

Jesus asked his disciples who and what they thought He was. Simon, who was usually more loquacious than the others answered, "You are the *Christ, the Son of the living God.*" The answer apparently pleased Jesus and He praised Simon saying:

> *"Blessed are you, Simon, Barjona (son of Jonah),*
> *because flesh and blood did not reveal this to you,*
> *but My Father who is in heaven."*
> **Matthew 16:17 (KJAV)**

Because I cannot believe that Jesus is partial, I cannot agree with commentators who suggest that Jesus had a special love for one of His 12 seminarians. It is possible that Simon has a unique charism. He was apparently the most loquacious of the twelve. Jesus tested Simon more thoroughly than he tested the others. He thrice asked him if he (Simon)) love him, and Simon ebulliently answered, "Yes, Lord" (John 21:15-19). Jesus gave him the charge. "Feed my sheep." Jesus issued an invitation to all the disciples, saying: "If any of you want to come with me, you must forget yourself, carry you cross, and follow me" (Matt. 16:24). He was apparently angry with Simon who pulled him aside to tell Him to stop talking about the suffering ahead. It was a harsh rebuke:

> *"Get away from me Satan! You are an obstacle in my way, because these thoughts of yours do not come from God, but from human nature."*
> **Matthew 16:23 (GNB-TEV)**

On the retreat, however, Jesus praised Simon's insight, and He christened or gave him the name "Rock," (Greek) "Petros" or Peter. That name was a good match for Simon's temperament. He was courageous. The Church of Rome teaches that Simon (Rock) was its first bishop and interpreted what Jesus said in response to his confession to suggest that Jesus built the Church on his (Simon's) charism. Even the erudite scholastic Thomas Aquinas seem to believe that Jesus laid the foundation of the Christian church on Simon. Much of what Jesus said about the future of His ministry was apparently addressed to the entire group of 12 disciples. He apparently empowered the twelve to bind and loose people from their sins.

Although verse 18 and 19 of the Gospel according to Matthew suggest that the key to the kingdom of God was given to Simon - with an implication that he specifically was empowered to forgive and retain the sins of the human race, a more careful reading of the verse 18 suggests the power was delegated to the twelve.

Simon was an organization man and Jesus probably delegated some organizational responsibility to him, but it is apparent that the church fathers assumed too much about Jesus' preference for Simon. Could the deference of the ancient fathers to Rome be a response to Rome's superiority in rhetoric? It is possible that because Rome was the center of imperial power until Constantine moved his capital to Constantinople, that the power of the emperor was projected on to the bishop of Rome. Cyprian of Carthage (mid-2nd century) thought so. Could the deference paid to Rome be the reason for the primacy of Simon (Peter) among the twelve? Was it the carelessness of the translators or intellectual dishonestly of the church in the west? Let us examine more closely the text that report the conversation of Jesus and his disciples near to Caesarea Philippi:

> *"And I say also unto thee, 'Thou art **Peter** and upon this **rock** I will build my church; and the gates of hell shall not prevail against it."* **Matthew 16:18 (KJAV)**

The above reply of Jesus is in three languages for greater clarity: English, Greek, and Latin. The key words in the text are ***Petros*** and ***petra***. They mean, ***Rock*** and **rock.**

English: *"You are **Rock** (**Peter**), and upon this **rock** (peter) I will build my church."*

Greek: "συ ει Πετροσ, και επι ταυτη τη πετρα οιχοδομησω μου την εκκλησιαν."

Latin: *"tu es **Petrus**, et super hanc **petram** aedificabo ecclesiam meam."*

The Greek **"Petros"** and Latin **"Petrus"** is a proper noun and means "Rock" in English. Note that the first letter "P or Pi" in the name is capitalized or upper case. The text continues; "and upon this **rock** (**petra**) I will build my church." The next rock (peter) is not a person but a thing. What thing?

The name given to Simon, or Simon's *Christian* name, is written with an upper case "P". It is masculine gender. The other peter is written with a lower case "p" and is neuter gender. Petra is a thing. **It is the confession of Simon.** The Christian name of Simon and the name of his confession are different nouns. Note also the noun endings. Greek and Latin masculine gender nominative case end in "os/us." Note that the neuter or feminine case ends in "a (am)." The name of the confession of Simon is "petra" **rock.**

Jesus looked steadfastly at Simon and said, "Simon! You are a **Rock/Peter (Petrus/os)** and I will build my church on this **"peter" (petra) (rock)**. The Christian Church is built on **the "petra" and not on the "Petrus."** The Church is built on the creedal confession, *"Jesus is Lord and Son of the Living God."*

John Stainer wrote a hymn that references Simon's confession.

*"My hope is built on nothing less. Than Jesus Christ, my righteousness, I dear not trust the sweetest frame, but wholly lean on **Jesus' Name**."*

The refrain is the creedal statement:

*"On Christ the solid (**petra**) rock, I stand; all other ground is sinking sand."*

The sacrifices of unblemished animals in the Jewish Temple at Jerusalem evolved to the self-sacrifice of the unblemished God-man (Jesus Christ) of Christianity. Some Christians believe that Jesus died as God (patripassionism)[cxxi] on the cross. Islam believes that He was only a prophet. Islam denied that Jesus was crucified and teaches that Jesus prophesied that God was sending another prophet that was apparently greater than him. Islam projected Mohammad or Ahmad) as that prophet.

The unrests in Christian and Muslims countries in the first and second decades of the 21st century have much in common. Christian theologians who advocate protests to correct past injustices including unjust socio-economic and political structures are referred to as Liberation theologians. Muslim advocates of revolutionary change are referred to as radical Islamists.

When Pope Benedict XVI, in an address at the University of Regensburg in 2006, said that Roman Catholicism is the sole mean of salvation, Muslims felt that it was an attempt to delegitimize the efficacy of their faith. Non-Roman Catholic Christians felt likewise. The Royal Al-Bayt Institute of Islamic Thought in Jordan issued an invitation to Christian and Muslim leaders to dialog. The title of the document in which the invitation was given is, *"A Common Word Between Us and You."* The theme-text of the dialog is,

> *"Say: O People of the Book! Come to a common word between us and you."* **Surah 3:64**

One hundred and thirty-eight Muslim leaders signed the invitation. It had three parts, namely:

a. The Scriptural basis for the call to love God in Christianity and Islam.
b. A common theme of loving the neighbor.
c. An invitation to Christians and Muslims to dialog.

Then Archbishop of Canterbury (Anglican/Episcopal) Rowan Williams, who had earlier participated in inter-religious conversations at non-sectarian venues in the United Kingdom, welcomed the opportunity for Christians and Muslims to explore the distinctive understandings of the two faith communities, especially their understanding of the person and nature of Jesus Christ. Citing Raimundo Panikkar in "The Trinity and the Religious Experience of Man," Williams suggests the following rational for dialogue among religious people:

> *"Is the discovery of how the Christian can intelligibly and constructively unite with the Buddhist or Muslim in the construction of the community of God's children rather than arriving*

at an agreed statement . . . there is no contradiction in a Trinitarian pluralism." cxxii

The National Council of Christian Churches in the United States of America, the Evangelical Lutheran Church in America, and the Presbyterian Church (USA) also welcomed the opportunity for dialog. Many Evangelicals were skeptical about rapprochement with Muslims. They felt that there was a hidden agenda. The Baptist World Alliance, Mennonites, and the Vatican were hesitant to respond to the invitation to dialog. The Southern Baptist Church cited theological differences and suggested that the Common Word dialog was Islam's attempt to "Islamize" Christianity.

The endgame of interfaith dialog is not to removal the boundaries of faith communities, but for mutual understanding of difference to enable understanding which may be a factor in peacemaking. Politicians who are motivated to power, invariably exploit religious difference to elicit sectarian support.

Roman Catholicism, which is a state—Vatican State—as well as a religious sect, has a religious as well as a diplomatic agenda. It endeavors to be consistent on both fronts. Despite the reticence of the magisterium periodically to engage in ecumenical and interfaith dialogue, some Roman Catholic colleges and universities engage interfaith staff. La Sallan Manhattan College, in Riverdale, New York, hired Mehnaz Afridi, a Muslim female, as an associate professor of Art and Director and head of its Holocaust Center. The same source reported that Chicago's Catholic Theological

Union hired Dr. Malka Simokovich as Chairperson of its Jewish Studies and director of the Catholic-Jewish Studies program.[cxxiii] Mainline Christian Protestant denominations have done likewise in their academies. Many donors view such progressive measures disapprovingly.

Although there are many positive engagements by moderate socio-political and religious Jews, Christians, and Muslims, the agenda of divisiveness and political extremism is fed to the world by the press. In a 1989 conversation with Ugandan clergy, one wonders aloud why the West embraced Dr. Milton Obote who was probably the cruelest of the Ugandan war lords. They opined that he was the darling of the western media and political power brokers because he was an educated Christian. General Idi Amin, to the contrary, was savaged because he was a Muslim. That may also be the cause of the hyper-negative rhetoric about radical Islam in the post-9-11 era. It may have boost media ratings, but it also encourages belligerence.

POSTSCRIPT

The Pew Research Center's tracking of the changing demography of Jews, Christians, and Muslims in the second half of the twentieth century and the first and second decades of the twenty-first century, project a faster rate of growth for Muslims than Christians. Muslim women are having more babies than Christian women per capita. Christian women gave birth to 33% of all the babies born in the years 2010 through 2015. Christian women of child-bearing age in those years was 31% of the aggregate population. Muslim women account for 31% of the births in that period, but Muslim women of childbearing age in those same years was only 24% of the aggregate population of the earth. The fact that Muslim women were having more babies per capita than Christian women is a probable reason for the increased activities of Pro-Life organizers in the USA in recent years.

The projected ratio of babies that will be born to Muslim and Christian mothers respectively in the years 2030-2035 is **225:224**; the projected ratio for 2055-2060 is **232:226.** The Pew Research Center also gives the following demographic of the earth's population in 2015 as:

a. Jews comprises 0.002% of the aggregate and 14,270,000 people.
   b. Christians comprise 31.2% of the aggregate and 2,276,250,000 people.
   c. Muslims comprise 24.1% of the aggregate and 1,752,620,000 people.

The demographic projection for 2060 is:
   a. Jews 16,000,000, which is 0.002% of the aggregate population of the earth.
   b. Christians 3,054,460,000, which is 31.6% of the aggregate population of the earth
   c. Muslims 2,987,390,000, which is 31.1% of the aggregate population of the earth.

The projection may change depending on:
   a. The rate of conversion
   b. Slower or greater growth of the Nones; people who do not identify with a faith community
   c. The opening-up of China to Christian evangelism
   d. Education and economic development

Conversion is a hot button issue in several countries. An estimated 10.2 million Muslims converted to Christianity in 2015. The number of converts from Christianity to Islam was not released. Intra-religious conversion—people moving between sects of the same faith, is common in the West. Christians change denominational affiliation. Christians comprised approximately 5% of the population of China in 2015. Should Christian evangelism have the same rate of success in China as it did in post-war South Korea, the percentage of Christians in China could increase precipitously. China currently has wide swathe of Islamic regions.

In a 2009 plebiscite in Switzerland to determine whether Muslin minarets should be permitted, 57.5% of the population voted to ban minarets on mosques. That political decision could spell trouble for Christians in the future. A Muslim majority in the future could ban the public display of the cross, crucifix, and Christus Rex. Religion ought to be the source of unity and not division. Catherine the Great of Russia reportedly embraced religious diversity, and Russian Muslims fought alongside Christians, Jews, and other religious sects in Russia's conflict with the Ottoman Empire. Vladimir Putin, president of the Russian Federation, cited the estimated 10 million Muslims residing in the Russian Federation in 2018, said that Islam and Orthodox Christianity have been Russian historical and cultural heritage. Like Catherine the Great, the Putin administration encourages Muslim immigration and subsidizes Islamic education and the building of mosques. Despite that rapprochement, there is a Chechnyan Muslim insurgency.

Jews in Russia are acknowledged as an ethnic community rather than a religion. An aid to Russia's Chief rabbi Berel Lazar, said that there is freedom of worship for Jews in Russia. He suggested that the Western media does not accurately report on religion in the Russian Federation.

The global population is being progressively secularized. Religious ghettos are shrinking as people integrate and learn the legends, myths, traditions, and religions of their neighbors. They are becoming more aware that what unites people is more powerful than that which divides them. That is both good news and bad news for religion.

Raimon Panikkar, a Catalan Roman Catholic priest of Spanish Roman Catholicism and Hindu parentage, is living out a new ecumenism. He went on a pilgrimage to India for inter-religious dialogue and discovered an interesting phenomenon. Returning to Spain, he confessed:

"I left Europe as a Christian, I discovered I was a Hindu and returned as a Buddhist without having ceased to be a Christian."

The judicatories as well as laity within religious communities are uncomfortable with that trend. In conversation with members of liberal as well as conservative congregations across denominations, I felt intense anxiety. Many confess feeling confused and sometimes traumatized by trends in the interpretation of the Scriptures. That renders them impotent to respond to what they believe is their call to evangelize. People are asking questions that are destabilizers of contemporary religion. "Is God male, female, or neuter gender? Is human sexuality relative to changing trends?" It is affecting Judaism, Christianity, and Islam, among the many religions competing for human attention. The ecclesiastical environment is becoming a war zone.

A Jew who did not identify himself as Orthodox, Liberal, or Reformed, expressed concern that people who are not grounded in the fundamentals of their faith will eventually join the rank of the Nones. Some Muslims express concern about the trend of inter-religion marriages. They see troubling implications of that trend for the faith formation of their offspring. I presided at the marriage of a Christian-Muslim couple and in retrospect regret that I did not encourage them to read the Judeo-Christian Scriptures and the Qur'an. I had not read the Qur'an at that point in my studies and ministry. They probably became secularized out of fear that to be religious as a Christian or a Muslim would be mutually alienating.

Some librarians in the public library systems report an uptick in requests for books on religion and philosophy. They do not know if that renewed interest in religion is reflected in increased attendance at synagogues, churches, and mosques. It may be a neo-Enlightenment. People ask librarians about Maimonides, Abu Hamid Al-ghazali, Thomas Aquinas, Richard Hooker, Soren Kierkegaard, Paul Tillich, Bishop Shelby Spong, and Pierre Teilhard de Chardin among other Jewish, Christian, and Muslim theologians.

The non-church going social scientist husband of a member of the parish I served in Chicago challenged me on a visit with the family to a debate on metaphysics. He said that he was beyond the Judeo-Christian Scriptures. I refused his invitation to debate. I could have told him that erudite philosophers had moved beyond metaphysics. His hurt feelings may have awakened spousal abuse when I left. The Christian church ought to resist debates about Jesus. The church is a bridge to faith, and Jesus Christ is the ultimate bridge to human unity.

The literature on Jesus Christ is available to everyone in print and on the electronic media. Laity as well as men and women in religious orders can compare the Church's canon of Scriptures with the so-called heretical books. Anyone can pick up copies of *The Secret Teachings of Jesus Recorded by His Disciples*, or the *Jesus Papers*, or Richard Carrier's *'On the Historicity of Jesus: Why We Might Have Reason for Doubt.'* Panikkar, Pierre Teilhard de Chardin, and Episcopal bishop John Shelby Spong may be the apparent post-modern "doubting Thomas'," but they are nonetheless soldiers of Jesus Christ. They have seen weaknesses in the medium through which the Gospel is transmitted to the faithful. They understand that Jesus is like stocks on the stock market: nurtured when the market is "bullish," shed when the market is "bearish," and they want to be better tellers of the good news.

ENDNOTES

i Joshua 10:1ff
ii Luke 1:31 New English Bible
iii Matthew 1:21, Ibid
iv John 1:1 & 14
v Acts of the Apostles 9:20
vi Isaiah 9:6-7; Jeremiah 33:14-14; Micah 5:1 & 2
vii On line Stuart Chase Brainy Quotes
viii The estimates have been borrowed from reports of the CIA.
ix Martin Buber, I and Thou, A new translation with a prologue and notes by Walter Kaufmann, (Charles Scribners & Sons, New York, 1970), p. 124
x Genesis 12:4
xi 'Abiru and 'Apıru,
xii Rev. John Topel, Liberation Theology: Explanation and Critique. This lecture was given at the University of Seattle on the occasion of the USA bicentennial Anniversary in July 1976.
xiii The Secret Teachings of Jesus: Four Gnostic Gospels (Book of Thomas) (Random House, New York, 1984), p.49.
xiv Rowan Williams, On Christian Theology, Blackwell Publishing, 2000), p. 225.
xv Rowan Williams, On Christian Theology, (Blackwell Publishing, 2000), p. 225
xvi Burton Scott Easton, translator into English, The Apostolic Tradition of Hyppolytus, (Archon Books, Cambridge University Press, 1962) p. 33. The issue that divides the Church in the Second Century was Christological; how to reconcile the strict monotheism inherited from Judaism with

the honors they gave to Jesus Christ. Hyppolytus suggested
that they follow the Logos doctrine of the Fourth Gospel.

xvii Cult is used here as reference to a mode of worship from "Cultus" (Latin) which means: "Honoring, reverence, adoration and veneration., Religious cults refer to the worship of particular religious groups.

xviii Amy-Jill Levine and Mark Zvi Brettler, (editors) The Jewish Annotated New Testament, (Oxford University Press, Revolt, A.D. 135, (

xix A. E. Taylor, Does God Exist?: An Essay arguing that it is unbelief, not belief that is unreasonable, (Fontana Books, Glasgow, 1961), p. 9 and 188.

xx Edward R. Hardy, Editor in collaboration with Cyril C. Richardson, Christology of the Later Fathers, in The Library of Christian Classics, Volume III," (The Westminster Press, Philadelphia), p. 107-108

xxi Theodore H. Robinson, Prophecy and the Prophets in Ancient Israel, (Gerald Duckworth & Co., 1963)., p. 19

xxii Leslie Dewart, The Future of Belief: Theism in a World Come of Age, (Herder & Herder, New York, 1968), p. 213.

xxiii William Kethe, paraphrase of Psalm #100, Hymnbook 1982, (The Church Pension Fund, New York, NY, 1985), #377

xxiv Pierre Teilhard de Chardin, How I Believe, Rene Hague, Translator, (Perennial Library/Harper & Rowe Publishers, 1969), p. 62 & 89

xxv Nathan Mitchell, The Amen Corner, Vol. 7, No. 3, May 1997 (Worship Magazine, St. John's Abbey, Collegeville, MN), p. 257.

xxvi Grant Gallicho, Simone Weil, In National Catholic Reporter, date February 13, 2004, (Kansas City, MO), p. 16 & 17.

xxvii Mary E. McGann, Timely Wisdom, Prophetic Challenge: Rediscovering Clarence R. J. Rivers Vision of Effective Worship, (Worship, Vol. 76, No. I, Collegeville, MN, 2002), p. 5 & 7.

xxviii Joseph T. Kelley, Donning the Mask and Joining the Dance: Religious Ritual and Contemporary Psychoanalysis, Worship,

ENDNOTES

	March 1998,Vol. 72, No. 2, (Liturgical Press, Collegeville, MN), p. 106-107.
xxix	Tony Robbins is a Motivational Speaker. The comment was made on a disc prepared at a workshop for business executives.
xxx	Deuteronomy 8:1 - 20. The Land is a gift and it was given with warnings of retribution should they disobey.
xxxi	Matthew 28:1-7; Mark 16:1-7; Luke 24:1-9; John 20:1-10.
xxxii	David Fagerberg, Chesterton on Liturgy, (Worship, Vol.71, No. 3, Collegeville, MN, ,), p. 198-203.
xxxiii	Mike Wilson, Editor, World Religion: Opposing Viewpoints,(Bonnie Szumski, Editor: Thompson Gale, 206),p. 213-215.
xxxiv	Francis Gonsalves, National Catholic Reporter, (May 28, 2004),
xxxv	Rene Teilhard de Chardin, The Phenomenon of Man, (Harper & Rowe Publishers, New York, 1965), p. 304
xxxvi	Acts of the Apostles 17:22-21 (KJAV).
xxxvii	The Laws of Biblical Israel were Codified in the Pentateuch or first five books of the Judeo-Christian Bible. The Decalogue is a summary of those laws. Referred to as the Mosaic Law because Moses was the supposed author, many had literary precedence in the 282 code of Law by Hammurabi of the First Babylonian Dynasty.
xxxviii	Mike Wilson, op. cit., P. 14
xxxix	Ibid., p. 203-210
xl	King Hammurabi of Babylon (Mesopotamia, died 1750 B.C.E. The 282 law Law Code was written on black slate. The Judaic Torah is similar to some of the laws of that code. It reflects a highly stratified society.
xli	Oesterley, W. O. E., A History of Israel: From the Fall of Jerusalem, 586 B.C. to the Bar-Kokhba (Oxford at the Clarendon Press, London, 1957), p. 129-130. A purpose of Ezra's Mission may have been to establish Orthodox Judaism in Israel. That Orthodoxy developed among the exiles in Babylon.

xlii	Elias Bickerman, From Ezra to the Last of the Maccabees, Schocken Books, 1962), p. 11
xliii	Ibid, p. 7
xliv	Max I. Dimont, Jews, God, and History, (Signet Book, New American Library, New Jersey, 1962). P. 168.
xlv	Rabbi Judas, The Oral Torah was a collection in 63 volumes which gave guidance on how to prepare kosher meats, travel on the Sabbath, etc.
xlvi	Ibid. p. 452-454
xlvii	This is a follow-up to a Law Suite of Jews For Jesus, et al, Appellants, v. Jewish Community Relations Council of New York, Inc., et al., Respondents, which was decided on February 25, 1992. Jew for Jesus want the Courts to cite Jewish Community Relations Council for breech of the law allowing Freedom of Religion.
xlviii	Oesterley, W. O. E., op. cit. 331.
xlix	Edmund Wilson, The Scrolls of the Dead Sea, (Collins: Fontana Books, London, 1963), p. 29.
l	Russell, D. S., Between the Testament, (SCM Press, Ltd., London, 1966), p. 53.
li	Bruice Chilton is the former Bernard Iddings Bell Professor of Religion at Bard College and Yale University in the USA and at Sheffield and Cambridge Universities in the UK.
lii	Max I. Dimont, op. cit., p. 40.
liii	Pinchas Lapide, Jewish Monotheism and Christian Trinitarian Doctrine: A Dialoge by Pinchas Lapide and Jurgen Moltman, Translation by Leonard Swidler, (Fortress Press, 1981), p. 37
liv	Ibid. p. 35
lv	The Orthodox Liturgy being the Divine Liturgy of S. John Chrysostom and S. Basil the Great According to the use of the Church of Russia, (Society for Promoting Christian Knowledge for the Fellowship of SS. Alban and Sergius, London, 1964),. 98
lvi	Richard Carrier, On the historicity of Jesus: Why we might have reason for doubt, (Sheffield Phoenix Press, Sheffield, 214), p. 107

ENDNOTES

lvii   A. Dupont-Somers, The Dead Sea Scrolls: A Preliminary Survey (New York: Macmillan, 1952), 99 and quoted by Professor Andrew C. Skinner of Brigham Young University in an on-line article (https://publications. Mi.byu.

lviii   Ibid., p. 337

lix   Ibid., p. 510-515

lx   Ibid., p. 390

lxi   Richard Carrier, op. cit., p. 282-5. (Richard Carrier is the rare scholar who shares salacious stories about the Holy Family of Christianity. Jewish anti-Christian sources put his birth about 100 years earlier than the Christian sources and suggested that his father was Panther or Pandera, a Roman soldier.)

lxii   Ibid., p. 283

lxiii   Henry Bettenson, Editor, documents of the Christian Church, (Oxford University Press, London, 1963), p.44

lxiv   Charles Brome Weigalls, Paganism in Or Christianity, (Charles Scribner's Sons, 1928), p. 136, 197-198)

lxv   Vladimir Lossky, The Mystical Theology of the Eastern Church, (James Clarke & C., Ltd., London, 1968), p. 247.

lxvi   Miriam T. Griffin, Nero: The End of a Dynasty, (Yale University Press, New Haven, 1984), p. 133

lxvii   Flavius Heroditus, Antiquities 18-20.

lxviii   Matt Slick, Online Reflection Regarding the quotes from the Historian Josephus about Jesus. Matt Flick is the President and Founder of the Christian Apologetics and Research Ministry.

lxix   Tacitus, Annals (written about AD 116), book 15, chapter 44. Printed on Wikipedia: Historicity of Jesus; a non-Christian and probable objective reference to the crucifixion of Jesus.

lxx   Alan Richardson, An Introduction to the Theology of the New Testament, (SCM Press, Ltd., London, 1958), p. 38 & 111.

lxxi   Harver Cox, The Secular City, (

lxxii   Pinchas Lapide, op. cit., p. 54.

lxxiii   Ibid., p.49.

lxxiv   Ibid. 49

lxxv	Jurgen Moltmann, The Trinity and the Kingdom, (Fortress Press, Minneapolis, 1993), p. 133.
lxxvi	J. N. D. Kelly, Early Christian Doctrine, (Harper & Rowe Publishers, 1960), p. 237.
lxxvii	A. R. Whitham, The History of the Christian Church to the separation of East and West, (Rivingtons, London, 1963), p. 198.
lxxviii	Colossians 1:15, "Christ is the visible likeness of the invisible God. He is the first-born Son, superior to all created things."
lxxix	Martin F. Connell, Heresy and Heortology in the Early Church: Arianism and the Emergence of the Triduum, in Worship, Vol. 72, # 2, (The Liturgical Press, Collegeville, MN, March 1998), p. 124-127.
lxxx	Ibid., 199.
lxxxi	Henry Bettenson, op. cit., p. 35.
lxxxii	Jurgen Moltmann, op. cit., p. 181. The Western Church wanted to stress the full divinity of the Holy Spirit.
lxxxiii	Ibid. p. 180. Russian historian and theologian Boris Bolotov hold contrary view of the procession of the Holy Spirit to that of other Eastern Orthodox, suggesting that the Holy Spirit proceeds from the Father only, but that the relationship of the Father and the Son makes the "Filioque clause" true.
lxxxiv	Ibid., p. 185.
lxxxv	Francis Young, The Making of the Creeds, (SCM Press, London, 1993), p. 71. The Nestorian apologetic, "The Bazaar of Heracleides" was found in the 1st or 2nd decade of the twentieth century.
lxxxvi	Jurgen Moltmann, op. cit., p. 163.
lxxxvii	Ibid., p. 63. This reinforces the reference of Frances Young to the "Bazaar of Heracleides."
lxxxviii	Joseph F. Kelly, op. cit. 44-45.
lxxxix	Leo Donald Davis, op. cit., p. 186.
xc	Nicolas Cheetham, A History of the Popes, (Barnes & Nobles Books, New York), p.34.
xci	J. N. D. Kelly, Early Christian Doctine, op. cit., p. 470 & 471.

ENDNOTES

xcii   Ibid., p. 154-158.
xciii   Henry Bettenson, op. cit., p. 127.
xciv   St. Augustine, The City of God, Vol. #2, John Healey, Translator, (J. M. Dent & Sons, Ltd, 1945), 386 & 387.
xcv   Leo Donald Davis, op. cit., p. 259.
xcvi   Ibid. p. 292-293.
xcvii   Ibid., p. 297.
xcviii Ibid., p. 310. Also Henry Bettenson, op. cit., p. 130.
xcix   Wikipedia, Ark of the Covenant, on line.
c   Pseudo-Dionysus: The Complete Works, (Paulist Press, New York, 1987), 220-221.
ci   Reza Aslan, No god but God: The Origin and Evolution of Islam, (Random House, New York, 2005), p. 117-118.
cii   Ibid., p. 41.
ciii   Ibid., p. 120.
civ   M. A. S. Abdel Haleem, The Qur'an, A new translation, (Oxford University Press, Oxford/New York, 2010), 169
cv   Ibid. 333
cvi   Faithful Neighbors: Christian-Muslim Vision & Practice, Edited by Robert S. Heaney, Zeyneb Sayilgan, Claire Haymes, (Morehouse Publishing, NY, 1916), 22.
cvii   Ibid, report by Munira Salim Abdulla and Gay Rahn. "Interfaith work and witness."
cviii   Ibid., p. 44
cix   Hans Kung with Josef van Ess, Heinrich von Stietencron, Heinz Bechert, Christianity and World Religions: Paths to Dialogue with Islam, Hinduism, and Buddhism, Translated by Peter Heinegg, (Doubleday & Company, Inc, Garden City, New York, 1986), 101-102.
cx   Ibid. 110.
cxi   Shahab Ahmed, What is Islam: The Importance of Being Islamic, (Princeton University Press, Oxfordshire, 2016), p. 48.
cxii   Reza Aslan, op. cit., p. 69.
cxiii   Hans Kung, op. cit., 125
cxiv   John Renard, Windows on the House of Islam, (University of California Press, Berkeley, 1998), p. 349.

cxv	Adonai, a Hebrew word which means Lord. It was written in the margin of Hebrew texts wherever the name YHWH appeared. Lectors read "Adonai" because it was inappropriate to enunciate the name of God (YHWH).
cxvi	Basilides, a Second Century Christian Gnostic who seceded from the Church at Rome after he was rejected as a candidate for bishop (Pope). He taught that Jesus was transfigured and assumed up to heaven and someone else was crucified.
cxvii	Ulrich Wilckens, Resurrection, Translated by A. M. Stewart, (John Knox Press, 1978), 104 -105.
cxviii	M. A. S. Abdel Haleem, The Qur'an: A New Translation, (Oxford University Press, Oxford/New York, 2008), p. 370.
cxix	Raymond William Baker, One Islam, Many Muslim Worlds: Spirituality, Identity, and Resistance Across Islamic Lands, (Oxford University Press, New York, 2005), p. 297- 309.
cxx	Judah M. Cohen, Through the Sands of Time: A History of the Jewish Community of St. Thomas, U.S. Virgin Islands, (Brandeis University Press, Hanover, 2004), P. 39 & 104.
cxxi	A. R. Whitham, op. cit., p. 146
cxxii	Rowan Williams, op. cit., p. 178.
cxxiii	National Catholic Reporter, (Kansas City, MO, November 16-29, 2018.), p. 5a.

AUTHOR'S BIOGRAPHY

The Rev'd Joslyn Lloyd Angus, Sr. is a naturalized citizen of the USA. He served churches in Jamaica, W.I.; Grand Cayman Island, BWI; Chicago, IL; Jacksonville, FL; and Savannah, GA. He served as adjunct instructor of History at Montego Bay High School for Girls, and Old Testament at Episcopal High School in Jacksonville, Florida. He also taught Caribbean Studies at the International College of the Cayman Islands, and was an Education Tutor with the Ministry of Education, National Youth Service Program in Jamaica.

His preparation for ministry includes: Studies at Mico University College and U.T.C.W.I. (Associate School of theology at the UWI), Kingston, Jamaica; B. D. University of London; M.A. (Church and Community) & Doctor of Ministry (Parish Revitalization), McCormick Theological Seminary; Anglican Studies, Seabury-Western Theological Seminary; PhD (Theology), Graduate Theological Foundation. He explored Eastern Orthodox Christianity in South-Eastern Europe on a travel grant from McCormick Theological Seminary; College of Preachers at Washington National Cathedral; Economics for Clergy, Bradley University; and Urban Ministry on a Lillie Foundation stipend at the School of Theology, University of Massachusetts.

He was a participant at the Caribbean Council of Churches in formation and the Caribbean Ecumenical Consultant for Development, Chaguaramus, Trinidad, in 1971; and did a month's mission trip to Uganda, E.A. in the summer of 1989.

He directed a non-secure juvenile pre-adjudication program in Jacksonville, Fl and a personal care home in Savannah, Ga. He was active in refugee resettlement ministry and served on the Florida Commission of Refugee Resettlement. He currently resides in Richland County, South Carolina.

PREVIOUSLY PUBLISHED:
Dynamic Christianity: The Impact of Pan-African Immigrants on the Church in the United States of America.

ISBN: 1-4259-1553-1 (SC)
Library of Congress #: 2006903083

www.ingramcontent.com/pod-product-compliance
Lightning Source LLC
Chambersburg PA
CBHW020122130526
44591CB00032B/342